YOWSAH! YOWSAH! YOWSAH!
The Roaring Twenties

Kenneth R. Bruce
De Anza College

Star
PUBLISHING COMPANY

Star

PUBLISHING COMPANY

P.O. BOX 68

BELMONT, CA 94002

Photos Courtesy of Wide World Photos
Cover Design: Debra Zink

Printed in the United States of America

SECOND PRINTING

PREFACE

ANOTHER BOOK ABOUT THE TWENTIES?

Objective and purpose are keystone words found in the teaching profession's lexicon. In teaching a survey course in United States History from 1920 to the present day, I find that as the years go by, the course gets longer and longer. In order to cover materials I feel are important in my classes I need more time as I usually run out of that precious commodity at the end of the quarter while discussing the United States' involvement in South East Asia (about 1968). This leaves the era of time from 1968 to the present uncovered and it is the era the students should hear about as it is their *own time*. Why? Because it gives students the opportunity to see and hear how they are becoming part of the grand scheme of history. It gives them a chance to see how they fit into the picture and it exposes them to the possible alternatives for their future.

To this end, I felt the only way I could accomplish the objective of reaching the present in my course was to cut something out. But what? To me each era of history is as exciting as the other. Rather than cut anything, I felt I could use other methods of instruction to accomplish the task of teaching the 1920s.

What method of instruction would I use? What information did I consider necessary for the student to know about the twenties? How could I immerse the student in that era of time so he could feel as if he was living then?

I decided to write a monograph on the twenties and include the information I felt would best give the student the feel for the era.

It was no easy chore, as anyone who has ever attempted to write a book can tell you. For the next four years I read and researched everything that was ever written by anyone on the twenties (or at least it seemed to me I did). I used periodicals, newspapers, books, films, recordings and scholarly articles written by other historians. From time to time I found a topic on the twenties so well written I felt it should be included.

Next came the task of putting all of the researched materials together in some coherent way so the student would know, feel, and understand what was happening in those days. With so many events happening at one time, and with each event an important overall contribution making the whole picture of the twenties clearer, I found that I had to criss-cross sections of history rather than put things in a concise chronological order.

During all my years of teaching, the one thing that has disturbed me more than anything else is the student who has a reading impairment or other problems with reading. Regardless of whose fault it is that "Johnny can't read," I felt that some method of instruction could be used to help those persons who had a problem with reading. I wanted them to learn about and enjoy the history of the 1920s which I was now setting down on parchment as much as other students and anybody else who might care to read *"my"* history of this era.

With this in mind, I turned my energies to recording on an audiotape that I had written. I narrated the tape and put music and sound effects with it. Many of my students contributed their voices and talent by portraying different characters of the 1920s, and I took original recordings from other sources so that when each tape was completed, a stereophonic effect of teaching and learning would take place with the listener and reader hopefully being that much richer in knowledge.

Enough said. I hope you will enjoy this book about the twenties, and that it whets your appetite to further examine history. Why? Because I believe that history really does try to teach us lessons on just about every subject if we will let it; for history is the source from which we learn to understand the present and plan for the future.

KRB

ABOUT THE TITLE

"Yowsah! Yowsah! Yowsah!" is a saying originated by Ben Bernie, who had an uninhibited gift of chatter as a band leader during the 1920s and 1930s. He was always gabbing to his audience and making up words and crazy sayings to get their attention. In fact, a book could be written just on his unending chit chat.

I selected the title when it was called to my attention by one of my students, and it *just seemed to fit.*

ACKNOWLEDGMENTS

To all who have put up with me for the past four-and-one-half years while I worked on this history . . . *thanks.*

Thanks also to some of my students who helped me track down many minute details.

Special thanks to the staff at the De Anza College Learning Center for getting the resources and materials I needed to put together this monograph, and in particular Mr. Gary Korn who found sources no one else could.

Extra special thanks to my copy-editor Mrs. Carol Miller for taking my manuscript and making it coherent and readable.

CONTENTS

Chapter 1
A DIFFERENT WORLD

It was 1920. The Great War, World War I, the war which was fought to end all wars was over and as the boys came home from Europe they found many changes. They found the United States which they had left was now *not the same.* Two new Amendments had been added to the Constitution. The first was the Eighteenth Amendment which dealt with Prohibition. For years antiliquor crusaders had been struggling to rid the United States of something called "Demon Rum." As they saw it, "Demon Rum" was responsible for all the ills of society. Do away with it and you end the problems which have forever plagued mankind. So when the boys got back from Europe, the strongest drink they got was soda pop. And as the song went, "How dry I am . . . how dry I am . . . I'd sell my shoes for a bottle of booze."

To back up the Eighteenth Amendment to the Constitution, the Congress of the United States passed something called the Volstead Act. This act said that the Internal Revenue Department would make sure that no illegal liquor would be sold throughout the country, and any product with over 1/2 of 1% of alcohol in it was illegal.

But as the saying goes . . . "You can lead a horse away from water, but he still wants to drink," or something like that. The fact was that the Eighteenth Amendment was not well liked by the people of the country. They wanted to drink and if the law did not allow it, they would drink anyway. But where could you purchase the booze? From a new kind of lawbreaker called a bootlegger. If the price was right the bootlegger sold you the liquor. Then too, speakeasies sprang up. A speakeasy was a place where the local citizens could get an illegal drink as well as entertainment of sorts. It seemed that everybody knew where the speakeasies were except the local police department as the "speaks" were seldom raided or shut down. The speakeasies did such a landslide business and made so much money that they bought off the police departments and corrupted city officials in high places with bribes to "look the other way."

Along with bootlegging and speakeasies came a new evil. It was something called organized crime. Prior to this time in American history, crime was a local thing, but bootlegging became big business calling for an organization not on the local level but on a nationwide level. And so the people of the country witnessed a struggle for gangland territory, and saw names like Al Capone, "Dutch" Schultz, "Buggsie" Moran, and a host of others hit the headlines in this era of violence. So. when you sum it all up, the Eighteenth Amendment was a failure. Instead of bringing an end to all our social evils, it brought forth the organized crime syndicate which the United States is saddled with today. And, as in the past, the reason organized crime can exist is because of you, the honest citizen. Yep! You're the one. As long as you place an illegal bet away from the track or purchase dope or support any other illegal enterprise, organized crime will be there to serve you.

The other amendment to the Constitution of the United States was the Nineteenth Amendment. This was the Women's Suffrage Amendment and it gave women throughout the country the *right to vote*. The Amendment came about only after a long struggle by the feminists of that era. These feminists were called suffragettes and they badgered and demonstrated until they had the right to vote. The most renowned crusader who promoted the Nineteenth Amendment was Susan B. Anthony. Although she never lived to see the amendment become law (she died in 1906), in her honor, many states have set aside February 15th as Susan B. Anthony Day.

But besides all of this legal mumbo-jumbo, the soldier returning to the United States also saw some style changes. Women's skirts were already six inches above the ground and going up. Indeed! The Nineteenth Amendment also seemed to do away with the hem line. Skirts prior to the Great War were down to the ground, and any young lady who showed any more than an ankle — well! She wasn't a lady. A young woman just wouldn't go about in such a flirtatious way showing herself to a man. It just wasn't done. But now skirts were so high that they became the joke of the day for many comedians. Probably the most used joke of the day was the story of Little Alfred. Little Alfred went shopping with his mother and got lost. The policeman who found him asked, "Lost your mother have you?" Little Alfred nodded yes. Then said the policeman, "why didn't you hold onto her skirt?" Little Alfred looked at the policeman and replied . . . "I cou-cou —couldn't reach it."

The brave new world of the 1920s also saw more and more aeroplanes flying around in the skies. Up to World War I the airplane was some kind of plaything, but during the war it became a useful machine. However, when the war was over no one could see much use for the contraption. The sad fact was that aviation probably would have died, and the advanced methods of travel we have today by super-sonic jets which cross the Atlantic ocean in less than three hours traveling time would not have been available to us

2

for another thirty or forty years. Two things saved aviation, "Barnstorming" and the establishment "Airmail" by the United States government.

Barnstorming was how some people made their living with a plane. A pilot and a friend of his, who was also an aviation nut, would show up at a county fair with their plane and for five dollars would give a ride to any daring person who would venture forth with the courage to fly.

If things got a little dull at the fair, the pilot and his nutty friend would take off in the plane and once in the air the pilot would do a few loop-to-loops to get the crowd's attention. Then his friend would get out and walk on the wing of the plane. Even though the crowds would marvel at the feats of this wing walker, you might well ask yourself what would happen to the poor fellow if he fell or was blown off the wing? In that case the wing walker would join the Caterpillar Club. Caterpillar Club? Yes! That was the name of the club that one could join if he saved his life by means of a parachute. The club was started in the early 1920s and a Lt. Harris of the United States Army Signal Corps was the first person to save his life by the use of a parachute. The term caterpillar club came about (if you haven't already guessed it by now) from the fact that parachutes were made of silk and silk is something which comes from a small creature called a caterpillar. It was the work of these early airplane stunt men and the men who carried the government's airmail that kept aviation alive.

By the end of the 1920s, aviation seemed to be getting off the ground and some people were talking about the fact that there were real possibilities in the idea of carrying passengers by air. If only a plane big and comfortable enough could be constructed to carry people, it might just work. It was done. Henry Ford of the Ford Motor Company fame built one of the best planes ever equipped to carry passengers in its day. It was the Ford Tri-Motor, which is sometimes affectionately called "The Tin Goose." It had two engines under its wings and one on the nose of the ship. The Tin Goose was designed by William Stout. It had thick wings, a corrugated metal body, and carried between eleven and twelve passengers. Its three engines were Wright whirlwind air-cooled radial engines, and each one would develop 420 horsepower. The inside of the plane was fairly noisy but the designers felt that the comfortable seats with their pillowed head rests would make up for the noisy sound. Furthermore, each seat was by a window which was curtained and each seat had an individual reading light. There was a braided silk hand grip for support in rough air, and for the first time a lavatory with hot and cold running water was put in a plane.

The first passenger flights across the country were done in stages. You

3

would take off from New York City and fly west until it started getting dark. As darkness fell, the plane would land somewhere around Columbus, Ohio. There the passengers would be transferred to a train and all through the night the train would head west. By morning the passengers would be in St. Louis, Missouri where they would load aboard another Tri-Motor plane which would be waiting for them. Again they would fly by daylight because the early planes were not equipped for night flying nor did they have all the instruments today's aircraft has for navigation. The pilot knew he was heading west by using a compass and he knew what route he was flying by looking from the window and following the railroad tracks which were only about 3,500 to 4,000 feet below him. Indeed, the passengers really knew they were flying and could at that altitude enjoy the scenery below. By nightfall of the second day the group landed near Amarillo, Texas. Again they would board a train and continue their journey until daylight brought them to Albuquerque, New Mexico. Now they boarded another Tin Goose for the last leg of their transcontinental journey.

The entire flight was made as comfortable as possible for the passengers by a young lady called a hostess. For lunch the hostess would serve the passengers sandwiches and for a hot beverage, she would serve tea or coffee from a thermos. Probably the most exciting part of the trip was when the pilot flew not over the Rocky Mountains, but through them! The plane could not fly over the mountains because the cabins were not pressurized like today's aircraft, and the passengers as well as the pilot had to breathe the air Mother Nature provided for them. As the plane went through the mountain passes, it seemed to the passengers that they could have reached out and scratched a match on the mountain's side. The low altitude combined with the air currents gave the passengers more than a thrill.

By the end of the third day the journey was over when the plane set down at Los Angeles, and what a trip it had been. Imagine crossing the country in less than 72 hours and moving along at speeds of 90 to 120 miles per hour. Is that traveling or is that traveling?

Besides the aeroplane, the 1920s also had more automobiles for us to get around in than we ever had before. There were well over 25,000,000 cars throughout the country and now you could even purchase one with a self-starter: a car that could be started by a battery rather than by a hand crank. It certainly was a relief to have a car you didn't have to start by cranking as there was great danger in starting a car with a crank. Why? After you had set the spark for the start, you had to go out in front of the car and begin turning the crank. If you had not set the spark correctly, the old car would backfire. The crank which was in your hand would fly loose — swing around — and break your arm between the wrist and the elbow everytime. Doctors during the 1920s did a big business resetting arms which had been broken by the unpredictable crank.

In the world of sports during the early 1920s, the "Manassa Mauler," Jack Dempsey became the heavyweight champion of the world. Sir Barton became the first horse in racing history ever to win the Triple Crown. Winning the Triple Crown in racing is done when a horse wins the Kentucky Derby, the Preakness and the Belmont Stakes all in one season. But the horse which captured the heart of the American racing fan during that era was Man-O-War. "Big Red," as he was called, ran up an impressive track record for his owners at Faraway Farms near Lexington, Kentucky.

In baseball, the Great American Pastime, sports writers were just uncovering something which would be known as the *Black Sox Scandal*. It appeared that the 1919 World Series had been thrown by eight players of the Chicago White Sox team when they played the World Series against the Cincinnati Reds.

As the series opened at Redland Park, which was the home of the Cincinnati Reds in 1919, the Chicago White Sox powerhouse was expected to trounce the weaker Reds in four consecutive games. The White Sox had Eddie Collins at second base and Ray Schalk as catcher. There was "Shoeless" Joe Jackson, a back country boy from South Carolina, who played left field and was idolized by every kid in the nation. He was described as a natural batsman and compiled a batting average of .356. There were other fine players on the team like "Shineball" Eddie Cicotte, an accomplished spitball pitcher and Claude "Lefty" Williams, a marvel of control on the mound. Oscar "Happy" Felsch was in center field, Gandil was at first, Charles "Swede" Risberg was at short and Weaver was at third. Not all the players were involved in throwing the World Series, only eight. They were Gandil, who was the ringleader of the sellout, Felsch, Cicotte, McMullin, Jackson, Risberg, Weaver, and Williams.

In the first game Cicotte took the mound and pitched against the Reds, who nine innings later defeated the powerhouse White Sox 9–1. From that moment on there was talk everywhere that gamblers had fixed the series and somebody on the Chicago team had been bought off, as the White Sox went on to lose the series.

A year went by with little evidence being found to substantiate the rumors. The only thing people had to go was gossip. Then in September of 1920, the whole thing broke loose. Jimmy Isaminger, a sports writer for the

5

Philadelphia North American broke the story. Billy Maharg, a friend of gambler "Sleepy" Bill Burns who had fixed the series, talked.

When the story broke the players involved in the scandal denied the whole thing. Then as the pressures mounted and troubled consciences became too much, pitcher Eddie Cicotte confessed that he and seven other members of the team had taken money from gamblers to throw the World Series of 1919. The scandal shook the very foundations of the Great American Pastime and it appeared baseball might not recover from the shock of it all.

Yet baseball did survive during the 1920s and has come down to us today as a sport which we all enoy. This was due to the influence of two individuals who gave baseball the wholesome look it needed after the Black Sox Scandal.

The first individual was Federal District Judge Kennesaw Mountain Landis, who was appointed by baseball to become its commissioner. He was to oversee that everything in the leagues was done properly from then on, and his first act as the Commissioner of Baseball was to bar from the sport forevermore the eight members of the Chicago White Sox team who had taken bribes even though a Chicago Grand Jury had acquitted the eight men of any wrongdoing. Judge Landis said, "Regardless of the verdict of juries,

Judge Kennesaw Mountain Landis (right) talking informally to Bill Terry of the New York Giants.

6

no player that throws a ball game or sits in a conference with a bunch of crooked players and gamblers where the ways and means of throwing games are planned and discussed, and does not promptly tell his club about it, will ever play professional baseball." The eight players involved in Landis' decision screamed, hired lawyers and got petitions signed but it was to no avail as none of them ever played in organized baseball again. Judge Landis, then, was the man who restored public confidence in the game by using strict discipline on both players and management as baseball never suffered another scandal. During his long reign as baseball commissioner, a post which he held until his death in 1944, he made such innovations in baseball as night games, lady's day at the ballpark, radio broadcast of games and he even developed the farm system for making professional baseball players.

The second individual who did so much for baseball when it was needed was George Herman Ruth. Ruth was known to every kid who grew up in the United States as the "Babe." He grew up in a Baltimore orphanage and went on to singlehandedly change baseball's form. Baseball up to Ruth's time was a defensive game characterized by the bunt, the squeeze, the steal, and the hit-and-run tactics. "Babe" Ruth changed baseball to an offensive game in which strategy was subordinated to sheer power as was represented by his home runs.

If the returning veterans were amazed by everything that was going on when they returned home from Europe, they must have been even more bewildered at the *Red Scare* which swept the country as they got back into their civilian clothes. The term Red Scare, as used by historians, related to the belief which was held by many people in the country that Communism was about to overthrow the government of the United States by force and violence.

The great Red Scare of 1919-1920 in the United States got started when a meeting of all the Communists in the world met in Moscow at the Third Communist International, in March of 1919. No sooner had the meetings of the Third International began than a Communist uprising in Bavaria and Hungary took place. This whipped up fears that bolshevism might engulf most of Europe and even the United States, for one of the boasts of the Third International was that "The United States was high on its list for revolution." Furthermore, Karl Radek, the executive secretary of the Third International, had boasted of sending money to Germany where a Communist group called the Spartacists were attempting to seize control of the new Wiemar Republic by force and violence. He also boasted that much more money was to be transmitted to New York City for the purpose of

7

spreading the revolution to the United States.

When the cost of living began to soar in 1920 to 105% above the pre-war level of 1914, it created a sense of irritation for the public, and it was just the sort of thing off which a Red Scare could feed. Then when a wave of strikes by workers, attempting to keep their salaries up with the rising prices took place, public opinion in the country became convinced that the nation was in the genuine throes of a Bolshevik revolution here in the United States.

Next came some bombings which confirmed suspicions that the revolt was coming. On April 28, 1919, Mayor Hanson of Seattle, Washington, who had just broken a dock strike, received a package in the mail. It was opened and was found to contain a homemade bomb which fortunately did not go off. An alert postal clerk who read about the incident in the newspaper suddenly remembered that he had set some sixteen such parcels aside because of insufficient postage. Bomb experts were brought in and sure enough, all sixteen parcels contained bombs. The bombs were disarmed and postal authorities throughout the country were warned to be on the lookout for eighteen more of the parcels which had been mailed. All eighteen parcels were recovered and destroyed. The people of the country were dumbfounded as to why these packages had been sent out to people like John D. Rockefeller, Judge Landis, and others. Newspapers speculated that the reason these men had received bombs was because they were looked on as the foes of labor.

Then Attorney General A. Mitchell Palmer's home in Washington, D.C. was bombed. The front part of his house was shattered and the bomb-thrower himself was blown to pieces by the blast. Enough evidence was found to indicate that the bomber was an alien and a known anarchist.

If all this wasn't bad enough, the Boston Police walked off their jobs and went on strike. Underpaid, overworked, and working under miserable conditions, they had voted in the summer of 1919 to affiliate themselves with the American Federation of Labor Union. Police Commissioner Curtis, a tactless overbearing man who hated unions, fired nineteen of the policemen who had joined the union. The angry men of the entire Boston Police Department then decided by an overwhelming vote to walk off their jobs and they did.

Most Americans now asked "How could they do this? How could they leave the city without any protection?" And inevitably, without any police protection, violence broke out in the streets of Boston. Shop windows were smashed, looting started, and before order could be restored two men were dead. At this point public opinion throughout the country strongly condemned not only this police strike but all strikes as well. Samuel Gompers, President of the American Federation of Labor Union urged the men to return to their jobs and let the issues of the strike be arbitrated. The police agreed, but Commissioner Curtis was determined to punish the strikers. He declared that no policeman would be reinstated and that he would recruit an entirely new force.

Gompers next wired the Governor of the State of Massachusetts Calvin Coolidge, who had done nothing during this strike, to take some action. Coolidge replied to Gompers in a terse telegram in which he said, "There is no right to strike against the public safety by anybody, anywhere, anytime." Within a few days the strike was broken and Coolidge's statement won for him great praise. Furthermore, in 1920 that statement also won for him the Republican Vice-Presidential nomination.

With all of this happening, the American people, already edgy over Bolshevism, bombings and labor militancy, began to view these incidents as an organized conspiracy to capture and control the government of the United States. They had come to believe that their country was faced by the menace of revolution, and all of this agitation led the people to demand that the government take action against these radicals.

The spotlight now shifted to the Attorney General of the United States, A. Mitchell Palmer. Palmer had been a loyal supporter of Woodrow Wilson ever since Wilson got the nomination for the Presidency in 1912. He was regarded by many as the father of badly needed child labor laws in the United States and he was also a strong advocate for the United States joining the League of Nations. In short, he was the prototype of a Wilsonian liberal. Besides all of this, Palmer had his eyes fixed at this moment in history on the upcoming Democratic nominating convention and as far as he could see there was a good chance for him to win that nomination.

Since the public wanted these bombings and strikes stopped, and since he was the Attorney General, he launched a series of raids which became known as the Palmer Raids. On November 7, 1919, members of the Union of Russian Workers in a dozen cities throughout the country were arrested and not long after that 249 aliens, who were believed to be the hard core of the anarchists, were deported from the United States.

With the anarchists gone, Palmer now turned his men loose on the Communists in dramatic coast to coast raids. If a person arrested was a citizen, he was turned over to state authorities for prosecution under anti-syndicalist laws. If he was an alien, he was deported.

Palmer invaded private homes, union headquarters and meeting halls.

9

People were held incommunicado, denied counsel and subjected to kangaroo trials. Perhaps at no other time before in the history of the United States had there been such a wholesale violation of civil liberties.

By the spring of 1920, Palmer had issued a series of warnings of a revolutionary plot which he said would be launched on May 1st, 1920. This, according to Palmer, was the first step toward the overthrowing of the United States government. To play it safe, Palmer had put major public buildings under guard, gave police protection to public leaders, called all state militias to the colors and put them on a 24 hour alert status.

The whole country waited for the fatal day. It came. But nothing happened. May Day passed without a single outbreak of violence of any kind. No shot was fired, nor were any bombs exploded. At this juncture of time, the country which had been scared out of its wits, became vexed at Palmer. He had cried "Wolf!" "Wolf!" once too often. And now the Congress of the United States turned its investigations on not the radicals but on Palmer.

Then on September 16th, 1920, during the lunch hour, a wagon load of bombs exploded on the corner of Broad and Wall Street in the heart of New York City and the financial center of the nation. Thirty-three people were killed, 200 were injured and many financial institutions were wrecked.

Palmer immediately began bellowing that this was the beginning of the Bolshevik conspiracy to overthrow the government, the very one which was supposed to have started last May 1st. A year earlier Palmer would have had the entire nation behind him, but this time the public, even though horror struck by the incident, took the event in stride. They felt that the bombing was probably caused by a group of demented anarchists.

By the end of 1920, the Red Scare was over. It was pushed to the back of the newspaper pages as the country took to reading more absorbing topics like the Chicago Black Sox Scandal. Yet, the Red Scare left behind a bitter heritage of suspicion of aliens, distrust of organized labor and a hostility towards reformers. Furthermore, the Red Scare would create a smothering atmosphere for reform efforts for the rest of the 1920s. Indeed, the Red Scare of 1919 which ended in the fall of 1920, would even cast a long shadow over the politics and policies of the 1930s.

But the big news in 1920 was — who would get the nomination for the Democratic and Republican parties and which party would be elected to office in November. As for the country, with its nerves rubbed raw by bitterness over the war, the debate on the League of Nations, the Red Scare, the labor disputes and the postwar inflation; it yearned for a release from the attacks of reformers and from the demands for altruism and self-sacrifice. In a word, the American people were weary of just about everything and wanted to loosen up and live.

To the professional politicans in the Republican party there was no question about victory in 1920. Therefore, they felt they could bypass strong-willed candidates and pick a weak party regular who would do their bidding. Up to this time there was very little public attention paid to Ohio's Senator Warren G. Harding. Yet, as early as February in 1920, Harding's campaign manager Harry Daugherty predicted that the strong candidates of the Republican party would kill each other off at the convention and Harding would eventually get the nod. When members of the press asked Daugherty if he really thought Harding had a chance he replied. "Well boys I'll tell you what I think. The convention will deadlock. Then some fifteen or twenty men, bleary eyed with lack of sleep, will get together in a smoke filled room . . . oh . . . about 2:11 in the morning. When that time comes, Senator Harding will be nominated."

It was not that the Republican party lacked for first rate candidates; on the contrary, they had men of stature like General Leonard Wood, Governor Frank Lowden of Illinois, and Senator Hiram Johnson from California. Then too, there was Herbert Hoover, who was known for his role in helping the people of war ravaged Europe, and Charles Evans Hughes who had been the Republican candidate in the election of 1916. Yet the Republican convention came extremely close to following Daugherty's script.

On Wednesday, June 8th, 1920, the Republican convention got underway in Chicago and by Thursday, June 9th, balloting began for the nomination. It soon became apparent that a deadlock would develop between the two main contenders, Governor Lowden and General Wood and sure enough it did. With the convention deadlocked a compromise candidate had to be sought. This was the time for Daugherty to trot out his dark horse candidate Senator Harding.

In the wee hours of Friday morning, June the 10th, just a little after 2 A.M., the party elders got together in a room at the Blackstone Hotel in Chicago and soon the room was filled with cigar smoke. There Senators Lodge, Brandegee, and Curtis along with a wealthy and influential magazine publisher by the name of Colonel George B.M. Harvey began to push Harding as the man to break the deadlock and to be given the nomination. It wasn't long until the other kingmakers in the room agreed. Yes, Harding would be the man! He would be the man they could control and he seemed to be the most malleable of all the second choice candidates. As Senator

11

Brandegee put it, "Harding . . . he's the best of the second raters." And so it was that about 2:09 in the morning, Harding was summoned to that smoke-filled room at the Blackstone Hotel. There Colonel Harvey addressed him point blank saying, "We think you may be nominated tomorrow. Before acting finally we think you should tell us whether there is anything that might be brought against you that would embarrass the party. Is there any impediment that might disqualify you to make you inexpedient either as a candidate or as President of the United States?"

Harding was shaken by the directness of Colonel Harvey's approach. He seemed almost stunned, and asked for time to think it over. He then withdrew from the smoke-filled room and after ten minutes of self-consultation, he reappeared and stated that there were no obstacles whatsoever. Harding felt he had done nothing great, but on the other hand he had done nothing to disqualify himself either.

Upon being assured that there was nothing in his past to hurt the party, the word was passed to the delegates on the convention floor and the next day on the tenth ballot Warren G. Harding became the nominee for the Republican party. When Harding accepted the nomination, he accepted it like a bewildered gambler, who was out of his class but who had won the big pot. He said, "Well! As they say, gentlemen, I guess we drew to a pair of deuces and filled . . ." His running mate would be none other than Calvin Coolidge, whose only claim to fame was that as the Governor of Massachusetts, he had made a succinct statement which had helped to end the Boston police strike in 1919.

So Warren G. Harding was nominated by the Republicans and one might ask, "How? How on earth did he ever become nominated by a political party and then get elected as the President of the United States?"

Harding was described as an idle boy, the son of a veterinarian who had turned doctor. He shirked any jobs of childhood, scamped on his education, quit teaching school in midyear because the work was too hard for him and eventually he purchased a dilapidated newspaper in Marion, Ohio. He next married a young lady named Florence Kling DeWolfe who was the daughter of the town mogul. She became the driving force behind him. Harding would probably have lived and died an unknown editor in a small town had one of his political speeches for a local office in Marion not been heard by Harry M. Daugherty, who was a political fixer at the state capital at Columbus. On the basis of Harding's flamboyant rhetoric and his distinguished appearance, Daugherty sought out Mrs. Harding. Between them, they got Harding elected to the Ohio State Senate. Harding was elected to the State Senate three times because of Daugherty's work, and eventually he got Harding elected as Lt. Governor. But when Harding ran for the governorship of the State of Ohio, he was badly defeated. Easily discouraged, Harding at this point in his career was ready to quit politics and return to being editor of the *Marion Star*. Both Daugherty and his wife kept after him to continue in politics, as there was a seat open in the United States Senate at this time. Would Harding run? Harding was reluctant after his defeat for the governorship but with persuasion, he ran and he won. He became a member of the most exclusive club in the world, the United States Senate.

As a Senator, he did almost nothing. Roll call found him present less than half of the time. When he was on the Senate floor at the time of a vote, he usually refrained from voting. He did not introduce one item of important legislation. But he was having the time of his life! There was the jovial companionship of the other more sportive Senators. There were golf games, prizefights, and baseball games to attend. There were poker parties, drinking parties, and pleasant company almost everywhere he decided to go. He had a mistress by the name of Nan Britton who would bear him a child, all of which would complicate his life as well as his reputation later on.

During Harding's tenure as Senator, Daugherty was patiently scheming to somehow get his man elected to the White House. Daugherty successfully maneuvered to have Harding present President Taft's name in nomination at the 1912 Republican convention and in 1916 Daugherty secured for Harding the temporary chairmanship of the Republican Party's National Convention where he delivered the convention's keynote address.

Now in 1920, Harry Daugherty believed that this year his man could win. Theodore Roosevelt was dead and Woodrow Wilson's idealism had soured in the public's mouth. The time was ripe for some second or third rater to make his move, and Harding did. He was in the right place at the right time to get the nomination of the Republican party.

As for the Democrats, they were in a quandary. Who could they nominate? Many leading democrats suggested that they ask Herbert Hoover (a republican) to run as their candidate. He seemed to be more of a democrat in his thinking than a republican anyway. Badly divided amongst several candidates, the democrats held their convention in San Francisco, and took 44 ballots before they picked Governor James Cox of Ohio as their presidential nominee. Franklin Delano Roosevelt who had been assistant Secretary of the Navy under President Wilson was selected as the vice-presidential candidate.

Before the campaign ever began, it was a foregone conclusion that

13

Harding would win. And by mid-October odds on the election were 7—1 in favor of Harding, which were the highest electoral odds ever given to that time in political history.

Harding hit the campaign trail and told the public things they wanted to hear as he spoke in vague and soothing cliches. For eight years the American people had heard Woodrow Wilson's sermons on duty, obligation, and national mission. They had responded to his appeals for domestic reform and his call to make the world safe for democracy. But now, now in the aftermath of the Armistice, things in Europe looked about the same as they did before the war. Not only that, but there was also a wide spread fear that a Bolshevik conspiracy would take over the country. Then too, labor unions in the United States went on strike to fight wage cuts and layoffs. Strikes were rather a new phenomenon to Americans, and after the Boston policemen's strike, which coincided with a sudden outbreak of anarchists' violence and bombings, the country was tired of hysteria and of being stirred up by politicians. What Americans wanted most was to get back to the business of making money and spending it, and Harding was the man who promised to "Return them to Normalcy." Normalcy? There is no such word. That is true, but Harding, who liked to bloviate, coined the word. He made it up and it caught on. In fact, it became his campaign slogan: "Back to Normalcy."

By election day everyone felt that Harding would win by a substantial margin, but no one anticipated the magnitude of his victory. On November 2, 1920, Americans for the first time heard the election returns broadcast by a radio station. The station was KDKA operated by Westinghouse Electric and Manufacturing Company in East Pittsburgh, Pennsylvania. This station became the first regular broadcasting station in the United States. As the station broadcast the vote, it revealed that Harding took 37 out of 48 states. Harding received some 16,000,000 votes to Cox's 9,000,000. As the democrats lamented, "It wasn't a landslide, it was an earthquake!"

Political scientists have since theorized that Harding won because he capitalized on the immense feeling of nostalgia for the ways things were in the United States before World War I — for the days when life was simpler. He swept the nation with his record vote because the people of the country were war-weary and impatient of problems too weighty for their minds to solve. Americans had also become cynically intolerant of the world's troubles and wanted to go back to the good old ways of living. So naturally they chose Harding as their spokesman to lead them back to the days of yesteryear.

There is no doubt that Harding was hopelessly miscast in the role of President of the United States. He had no qualifications for the Presidency except for the fact that he looked like a person who could be President. He was handsome, gray-haired and had a splendid figure. He was kindly, companionable, free of graft, and had a winning personality. He was warm and lovable and had a limitless store for liking people. Of statesmanship, he had none, nor did he ever profess to have any. He knew nothing of history, economics or sociology. He was neither educated nor informed on anything. He was devoid of ideas and shrank away from most problems, as he knew they were beyond his powers to solve.

He was a member of the Elks, the Odd Fellows, the Hoo Hoos, the Moose, and the Red Men lodges. Unfortunately, his friendly sociability proved to be his undoing, for in little or no time at all his friends began to take advantage of his good naturedness and his administration soon became an administration governed by political hacks and cronies.

Yet Harding, who acknowledged his limitations, announced he would surround himself with the best minds available in his cabinet to help and guide him. To that end he appointed Charles Evans Hughes as Secretary of State, Herbert Hoover as Secretary of Commerce, Andrew Mellon as Secretary of the Treasury and Henry Wallace as Secretary of Agriculture.

Then there were Harding's friends or cronies who were also appointed to government offices and who would rob him of his good name. First there was Secretary of the Interior Albert B. Fall. He had been a friend of Harding while he was in the Senate. Next there was Harry M. Daugherty, the man to whom Harding owed his success; the man who got him elected from the state level all the way to the Presidency. For his reward, Daugherty took the position of Attorney General. It was a position from which he would sway and misguide the President.

Nevertheless, with a cabinet like this, one might yet ask, "How could Harding really go wrong?" Certainly the integrity of men like Hoover and Hughes was incorruptible. They could give the President excellent advice. But that was the problem. These men were of such high caliber, and so brilliant in thought, that they spoke a language which the President could not understand. He wanted to understand, but it was too much for him. So, he would just sit in his cabinet meetings looking bewildered.

There were grave issues which needed remedying. Issues like unemployment, national financing, taxation, tariff adjustments, lawlessness coming out of the Prohibition Amendment, the peace treaties and the League of Nations. But since Harding was not at ease with the intellectuals of his

15

cabinet, he rarely called a meeting. Instead, two or three times a week, he would get a group of his old buddies together at the White House for a poker game. Harding managed to establish in the White House the same atmosphere which permeates any backroom saloon where gambling takes place.

President Harding and his cabinet. Seated, left to right, Secretary of War John W. Weeks; Secretary of Treasury Andrew W. Mellon; Secretary of State Charles E. Hughes; President Warren G. Harding; Vice President Calvin Coolidge; Secretary of Navy Edwin Denby. Standing: Secretary of Interior Albert B. Fall; Postmaster General Will H. Hays; Attorney General Harry M. Daugherty; Secretary of Agriculture Harry C. Wallace; Secretary of Commerce Herbert Hoover; Secretary of Labor James J. Davis.

It would be unjust to say that Harding deliberately shirked his work. He was not lazy nor was he indifferent. He just couldn't seem to grasp the fact that he was the President of the United States nor did he really know what to do. So, he went back to the genial companionship of the Poker Cabinet where everybody was so comfortable and no questions arose to put a strain on his mind.

At these poker parties one would surely find Fall and Daugherty. Then, there was Charley Forbes, an old friend of the President. Harding liked him because of the jokes he told and appointed him as head of the Veteran's Bureau. Next, there was Ned McLean, a millionaire and society man, but who, as Harding put it, was not a bit stuck-up about it. Besides attending the meetings of the Poker Cabinet, McLean also gave long night parties. He was one person with whom the President found real mental relaxation. Then there was "Doc" Sawyer, Harding's personal physician who came from Harding's home town in Marion and who played a stiff hand of poker. "Mort" Mortimer was also there. He was the President's personal bootlegger and knew where the best liquor was to be found. He kept the President and his friends well supplied with all the liquor they could drink. But . . . but . . . wasn't that against the law? Didn't the Eighteenth Amendment forbid the consumption of alcoholic beverages? Yes it did. But to heck with those bluenoses who didn't like drinking people! This was a great bunch of guys and President Harding was right in his element. There was no doubt about it either, as the White House was filled with his cronies and the air was heavy with tobacco smoke. Trays with bottles containing every imaginable brand of whiskey stood about the place. Cards and poker chips were readily at hand, and a spitoon sat alongside the poker table.

From the beginning reporters in Washington were aware of the moral laxity taking place in the Harding Administration, but they said very little about it. Farther downtown from the White House the undercover business of the Harding Administration was going on, and it was done strictly on a "cash and carry" basis. At a dwelling at 1625 K Street (known as the Little Green House) there seemed to be a continuous celebration. Cardgames were always in progress; the bar never closed; girls came in and went out on call; underworld figures met with politicians to discuss such matters as pardons, paroles, and withdrawal certificates which permitted the purchase of alcohol for "industrial" or "pharmaceutical" uses. Then too, a person could purchase an appointment to office or get an illegal concession such as immunity from prosecution. Anything anybody might want out of the government could be purchased. The only question was . . . how much?

The hosts of the "Little Green House" on K Street were Howard Mannington and Jess Smith. Mannington held no office in the government but was an old friend of Harding's and was an inner member of what was called the "Ohio Gang." Jess Smith was the liaison man between the Department of Justice and the "Little Green House." He was a pulpy, sputtering, loose-lipped, sportily dressed individual who loved to loll around greeting people with stale jokes and stock queries. Jess operated in two worlds. One world was the minor graft of K Street and the other world was the large scale operation of graft which was sponsored by his boss Attorney General Harry M. Daugherty. He and Daugherty lived in a rent free house of Ned McLean's on a 50,000 dollar a year scale while only making 12,000 dollars salary a year. In short, Jess was the man to see when one had ready cash to pay for an office or buy a favor. As the Washington newspaper men put it . . . "Jess ran the Department of Easy Virtue" and for more than two years Smith and his confederates lived high on the hog.

As for Charles R. Forbes, the man Harding appointed Director of the Veteran's Bureau, he also promptly cashed in on his opportunities and became a notable figure in the night life of the capital. Lavish entertainment was the order of the day and Forbes outdid everybody else with his parties. Furthermore, he did all of this on a salary of 10,000 dollars a year! Nobody seemed to question where he got the extra money on which he lived so grandly, as asking questions was not considered good form during Harding's Administration. Forbes got his money by making deals with construction companies who wanted the fat contracts to build veteran's hospitals which were being constructed throughout the country. If a construction company agreed to grease the palm with enough money, Forbes would see to it that they got the contract. Then too, at a time when disabled veterans were lying on hospital cots needing bandages, bedding, and drugs, Forbes was condemning carloads of these veteran's supplies and selling them off at a fraction of what they had cost the government. To a Boston concern he sold some $3,000,000 worth of these needed supplies for a neat rake-off of $600,000. All in all, in less than two years time, Forbes had cost the American taxpayers well over $200,000,000.

While all this was happening at the Veteran's Bureau, looting on a grander scale was in progress down at the Department of the Interior. There Secretary of the Interior Albert B. Fall badly needed money. He owned a ranch in New Mexico which was rundown and had nine years of back taxes due. To raise money, Fall leased United States oil reserves to a couple of big time oil men for a price. Instead of calling for competitive bids from all oil companies to develop these oil fields, Fall let Edward L. Doheny, the President of the Pan-American Petroleum Company have the government oil reserves at Elk Hills, California for $100,000 which went right into his pocket. The money was transferred in a briefcase to Fall by Doheny's son. Next, Fall leased (again without competitive bidding) the oil reserves at Teapot

Dome, Wyoming to Harry F. Sinclair of Mammoth Oil Company for about $125,000.

All of a sudden the back taxes on Fall's ranch were paid. Its rundown condition was taken care of as the ranch was put back into shape and stocked with prime blooded cattle. Indeed, prosperity had smiled on the Falls and most people were amazed that Fall was able to accomplish this with only his salary of $12,000 per year.

By the end of 1922 and the beginning of 1923, more and more newspapers were becoming extremely critical of Harding's leadership. All of this was getting under the President's skin. Then, to add to his distress, Harding had family complications, as Mrs. Harding was beginning to suspect her husband's conduct with Nan Britton who had been slipping through the side door of the White House to see and console the President at night. Suddenly Mrs. Harding confronted her husband and his mistress, and after a nasty scene, Nan Britton was packed off to Europe at the President's expense.

With all of these vexations, the President slept badly and rose in the mornings unrefreshed. In fact there was a serious concern about his health. Perhaps what the President needed was a change. Well then, why not take a trip and take some friends along? Go see some new country like Alaska and take a vacation away from official speeches. He could go out in the country and bloviate. Indeed, the President would enjoy doing this and with his friends Ned McLean, Mort the bootlegger, Charlie Forbes, Harry Daugherty, and Jess Smith, it would be a jolly junket. His good friends could always be relied upon to divert his mind from the burdens and irritants imposed upon him as President.

In the midst of planning his trip, the first of many scandals which were to rock the nation broke loose. The affairs of Charlie Forbes (Director of the Veteran's Bureau) hit the press. The evidence of his corruption was overwhelming. So bad was the scandal that Forbes' right-hand man in the Veteran's Bureau, Charles Cramer, who was also deeply involved in the veteran's graft, committed suicide in March of 1923.

It wasn't long after this incident that Forbes was called before the President. Harding was exasperated at the fact that one of his friends had sold him out. Highly overwrought, as he was upbraiding Forbes, the President grabbed him by the tie, jerked him up close, shook him like a rag doll, and at the same time yelled out the only words that came to his mind, "You dirty rat . . . you double-crossing bastard!"

This scandal was Harding's first positive disillusionment. He had always

19

been a confirmed optimist, but now he began to find out that Forbes' disloyalty was not just an isolated incident. He began to learn that most of his buddies were destroying his name, that there was a general condition of rottenness throughout his administration, and that too many people were keeping information from him.

At this point, Harding sent for Jess Smith. As he put the screws to the pulpy grafter, Smith broke down and in his slobbering, sputtery speech, he told Harding what the President feared he would — what had been concealed from him for more than two years. After it was all over, Harding said to Smith, "Go on home now, Jess, and get a good night's rest because tomorrow you'll be arrested." Jess returned to his hotel suite which he shared with his crooked boss Daugherty, and there he blew his brains out with a pistol.

All of this shocked Harding into personal reform. The White House poker parties came to an end. He told his friends he was off liquor. Furthermore, he lost his taste for revelry and the plans for his Alaska trip were radically revised. Instead of a trip to make whoopee, it was now scheduled as a serious political mission and his old crony friends were not invited to go either. Instead, other men of respectability were asked to go on the trip. Men like Secretary of the Interior, Doctor Work (he replaced Fall), Speaker of the House of Representatives Gillette, Secretary of Agriculture Wallace, and Secretary of Commerce Herbert Hoover were now asked to accompany the President.

Hoover joined the President at Tacoma, Washington with some good news which the President announced to the press. After long negotiations between labor and management. Hoover was able to get the steel industry to give up the 12 hour day (84 hour week) and accept the idea of giving its workers an 8 hour day (48 hour week).

Once the announcement was made to the cheers of the laboring people, President Harding became a man with a chronic state of jitters. He could not be quiet for five minutes at one time. What he was trying to do was escape from thinking. To this end he organized a bridge game going to and coming from Alaska aboard the Navy's transport ship *Henderson*. The President played twelve to fourteen hours a day until he was exhausted. The game started immediately after breakfast and went on well into the next morning with only a brief break for lunch and dinner. The other players took turns and played in shifts. Herbert Hoover, after this dismaying experience, never again played the game of bridge.

While on the trip Harding sought the advice of Hoover on what to do about the scandals which were brewing in his administration. Hoover told

Harding to open up the scandals without delay and let the people know what was happening. Harding stared at Hoover unhappily. It was not the advice he had hoped to hear. He was hoping there was some other way. But after thinking it over, he knew it was the only thing to do. When he got back to the capital, he would air the scandals publicly.

On the way back from Alaska, the President stopped over in Vancouver. There on a stifling hot day, Harding went about in an open touring car making speeches. Reporters who had gone along on the trip were quick to notice that the President seemed listless and that his delivery was flat and dull. Was there something wrong with the President?

In Seattle, Washington, Daugherty, the man who had taken Harding from a small town politician and made him President, joined the Presidential party. As Attorney General under Harding, Daugherty had also sold out the President. After a long talk behind closed doors, Daugherty told the President of more scandals which were about to break out in his administration. When the President emerged from the conference with Daugherty, his face was drawn and Daugherty scurried away like a rat in light.

Harding's will to live now seemed to be broken by this last conversation. Forbes, Fall, Daugherty, and all the other old cronies of the "Ohio Gang" had betrayed him. Who could he trust now? Whom could he turn to for advice? The President was helped back to his train, quivering, nervous, and looking extremely ill. His doctor, "Old Doc" Sawyer, diagnosed the President's condition as acute indigestion caused by some crab meat the President had eaten. Yet, other members of the party who had eaten the crab meat had not suffered any ill effects.

As the Presidential train headed toward San Francisco, Dr. Boone, a physician of wide experience and high standing examined the President along with Dr. Work. Both were convinced on completion of their examination that the President was not suffering from indigestion but was suffering from a coronary thrombosis, the symptoms of which resemble a sharp upset stomach.

Specialists were on hand to meet the President's train as it came into San Francisco. There Harding was told the seriousness of his condition and for a few succeeding days the President worsened. Then he began to feel better and while it looked as if he would recover, pneumonia set in. The weakened heart made it difficult to clear his lungs. Despite all of this, it still looked like the President might make it through his difficulties. Then as he was recovering, and while his wife was reading a magazine article to him as he lay resting in bed, a wandering blood clot struck his brain. The President died instantly.

21

The cortege across the nation to Washington, D.C. and thence to Ohio where the President was buried saw unparalleled throngs of mourning and weeping people. For that brief moment of time Warren G. Harding was the well-loved President he had hoped to be.

It took years to clean up the debris which was the legacy left by the Harding Administration. The public held its nose over the rising stench of the scandals. Forbes went to jail as did Fall and Sinclair. Daugherty, the biggest crook of them all, escaped jail, however, thanks to two hung juries.

As for the dead President, his personal life did not escape the afterwave of scandal either. Nan Britton published her book in 1927 entitled *The President's Daughter*. It was a book of sordid intrigue, beginning with thirty dollars tucked into Nan's stocking top and ending with her affairs with Harding in the White House. It shamed and nauseated the country as the American people now asked nothing better than to forget Harding and anything that was associated with him.

Then too, Gaston B. Means wrote a book which bore every imprint of being a fake. In his book *The Strange Death of President Harding*, published in 1930, Means charged in so many words that Mrs. Harding poisoned her husband in sort of a mercy killing to save him from impeachment which she foresaw.

Historians have said of Warren Gamaliel Harding's administration, that without wanting to, knowing of, or trying to do anything at all unusual, he became the figure head of the most flagrantly corrupt regime in the history of the United States in the first half of the twentieth century.

Chapter 2

TRANSITION—FROM HARDING
TO COOLIDGE

Despite the fact that the Harding Administration reeked with corruption, some positive steps towards world peace were taken by the United States to see to it that her sons would never again have to go forth and fight a war like World War I. This point was driven home on November 11, 1921 (which was the third anniversary of the signing of the Armistice which ended World War I). It was on this third anniversary that the solemn burial of America's Unknown Soldier at Arlington Cemetery took place.

After World War I there were over 2,000 American doughboys buried in France whose very identity had been obliterated by battle. The people of the United States had expressed no formal national feeling of any sort since the end of World War I to show their appreciation for the sacrifices made by their young men. Many Americans now believed that the most fitting way to honor these men who had gone to war, and for those who had made the supreme sacrifice in the war, was to bring one of those unknown soldiers from France and bury him in the United States. This Unknown Soldier would typify the soul of America and the sacrifices made by all.

The original idea of honoring one Unknown Soldier for all was that of a Frenchman by the name of Francois Simon. His idea swept halfway around the world to the United States, where it was felt that any mother who had lost a son; or wife who had lost a husband, and whose body had not been or could not be identified, could stand at the tomb of this Unknown Soldier and think that the body of the soldier there interred, might be her loved one.

So it was that from each of the four cemeteries where American soldiers were buried in France, an unidentified body was selected. He was an unidentified American doughboy who had died to make the world safe for democracy and who had fought a war which was to end all wars forever. Unmarked coffins containing the unidentified bodies were next lined up and Sargeant Edward Younger, a highly decorated veteran of World War I was selected and given the honor of making the final choice as to which unidentified soldier it would be. With high government officials watching and soldiers standing at attention, Younger walked down the row of flag-draped caskets. Then, he stopped and touched one of the coffins. That unidentified American would become the one Unknown Soldier who would represent all.

No President, no national hero ever went to his final rest with the honors given our Unknown Soldier. To him went the Congressional Medal of Honor, the Distinguished Service Cross, plus the highest decorations from other countries; Great Britain, France, Belgium, Italy, Rumania, Czechoslovakia, and Poland.

There at the solemn ceremonies were ex-Presidents Taft and Wilson as well as President Harding. Furthermore, General John J. Pershing who commanded the American Expeditionary Forces in Europe was also present. Walking behind the gun carriage which bore the casket were not only dignitaries from the United States but dignitaries from other countries as well. The procession made its way across the Potomac River to Arlington National Cemetery. There America's Unknown Soldier was laid to rest, while prayers were offered with the hope that it would never again be necessary to shed blood in another world war.

President Harding paying tribute at the casket of the body of the Unknown Soldier.

After the ceremonies were over a lone sentry took his post, and from that time to this a sentry has always guarded the tomb of the Unknown Soldier. It has been said that it is easier to get into West Point than to become a member of the honor guard that performs the 24 hour a day guard duty at the Tomb of the Unknown Soldier. Each of the sentinels patrols one hour per day. During this hour, the sentinel walks his post at strict attention.

He will walk his post exactly 42 times. He walks precisely 21 steps from one end of his post to the other. He faces the city of Washington, D.C. exactly 21 seconds; faces the Tomb of the Unknown Soldier 21 seconds; and carries his highly polished rifle with a fixed bayonet, keeping the rifle always on the shoulder away from the tomb. This symbolizes that he has placed his body between the Tomb of the Unknown Soldier and all danger. The 21 count and the 21 steps from one end of his post to the other symbolizes the 21 gun salute given all persons of high honor.

Later on — on Memorial Day 1958, an unidentified soldier from World War II and the Korean War were buried in a marble-capped crypt at the head of the original tomb. Each year millions of tourists watch the changing of the guard at the Tomb of the Unknown Soldier and pay tribute to a person who gave his life for the ideals in which his country believes . . . *FOR HERE RESTS IN HONORED GLORY AN AMERICAN SOLDIER — KNOWN BUT TO GOD.*

It was the day after the solemn ceremonies of the burying of the Unknown Soldier that the Washington Naval Disarmament Conference took place. One of the causes of World War I was an armament race between the great powers of Europe. Most political scientists agree that the armament race led to a group of nations bristling with firepower and eventually someone decided to use it.

With World War I behind it, a naive America, concerned about the possibilities of a new arms race, especially in naval armament, felt that history should not repeat itself. To this end, the United States worked toward getting the world powers together to head off any such armament race. Besides, building battleships was an expensive business and most of the people in the country felt that federal expenditures should be kept low.

The initiative for the naval disarmament conference came in early 1921 when Senator Borah of Idaho introduced a resolution in the United States Senate, suggesting that the President take the initiative and call such a conference. The resolution passed and invitations were sent to all the major powers of the world asking them to send representatives to the conference which was to be held in Washington, D.C. The major world powers attending the conference which got underway on November 12, 1921, were Great Britain, Japan, France, Italy, China, and the United States.

President Harding opened the first session with a cordial, profuse speech of welcome. Then true to his policy of leaving difficult problems to be solved by the "best minds," he turned the conference over to Secretary of State Charles Evans Hughes. Hughes had a brilliant mind, a definite plan, and

25

a masterly grasp of the complicated issues at stake.

President Harding had hardly walked out of the Memorial Continental Hall, where the conference was taking place, when Secretary of State Hughes, who was the chairman of the conference, took the rostrum and began to speak. Most of the delegates settled back in their chairs to listen to what they believed would be the usual perfunctory remarks which are expected of a presiding officer. As Hughes began his address, the delegates nodded to acquaintances around the room while others smothered yawns. But to the surprise of the delegates, Hughes skipped all the opening mumbo-jumbo and electrified them with this statement: "The only way to disarm is to disarm." The assembled delegates about the long conference tables came alive when to their amazement, Hughes laid before them a definite and detailed program. There was no beating around the bush and no waiting for the cocktail hour. Hughes was there to get something accomplished between the nations . . . and that was disarmament. Hughes proposed a ten-year naval holiday, during which no capital ships (battleships and battlecruisers) would be built. Furthermore, there would be an abandonment of all capital shipbuilding, and the scrapping of ships which were already constructed and being constructed. He went on to name the 33 American battleships which would be scrapped, told the Japanese and the British just what ships in their navies he expected them to scrap.

Admiral Beatty, the British Admiral who had defeated the German navies at the Battle of Jutland in World War I, almost fell out of his chair at the conference when Secretary of State Hughes declared that Britain should stop construction of its four new battlecruisers and demanded that the battleship *King George V* be sunk.

Next Hughes went on to say that the limitation of replacements of all capital ships should be according to a 5-5-3 ratio. The American and British navies would be kept at parity and the Japanese fleet would be held to 3/5 the size of the British and United States fleets.

Hughes concluded his remarks by saying:

"With the acceptance of this plan, the burden of meeting the demands of competition in naval armament will be lifted. Enormous sums will be released to aid the progress of civilization. At the same time, the proper demands of national defense will be adequately met and the nations will have ample opportunity during the naval holiday of ten years to consider their future course and preparations for offensive naval war will stop NOW."

Hughes' speech was an absolutely unique diplomatic episode and it was greeted by a torrent of wild cheering as delegates waved their hats, yelled, jumped up and down, and hugged one another. The prolonged applause was echoed throughout the country by the press and around the world. The imagination of the people of the world was so stirred by the boldness of Hughes' plan that the success of the conference was almost inevitable.

When the cheering and applause was over, however, and the business of serious negotiations took place, it appeared that Japan was reluctant to accept the short end of the ratio. Japan had come out of World War I as one of the great powers of the world. The German island possessions in the Pacific were given to Japan for her aid in the war against the Central Powers. In order to placate Japanese fears that the United States or Great Britain would attack her in her part of the Pacific, Hughes concluded a separate agreement with Japan and England which was known as the Pacific Demilitarization Agreement. The agreement stated that the United States would not fortify any of its possessions in the Pacific west of the Hawaiian Islands, and England agreed not to fortify any of its possessions in the Pacific north of Singapore. With these assurances, Japan agreed to go along with the 5-5-3 ratio Hughes had established.

After three months of negotiations, the Disarmament Treaty of Washington was signed. The disarmament treaty, along with two other agreements which became known as the Four Power Pact and the Nine Power Pact, not only limited the construction of capital ships it also outlawed the bombing of civilian objectives and the use of poison gas and dum-dum bullets in any future wars.

From the positive side of things the Washington Naval Disarmament Conference succeeded in halting the construction of capital ships which was more than any other disarmament conference in history had been able to do. It reduced tension in the Far East and it provided one of the most hopeful atmospheres for peace throughout the world, for without halting an arms race there was little hope of settling things diplomatically. The conference also showed that the armaments which were built by a nation were now a matter of international concern to all nations and should be subject to world control.

Nineteen years later, however, the folly of the Washington Naval Disarmament Conference would come home to roost and show a naive United States that some countries do not always abide by treaties. In retrospect it is easy to see what this foreign policy established in the 1920s did. In 1941, the Japanese attacked the United States Fleet at Pearl Harbor and then went on to take over most of the Pacific. How? How could Japan do all of this in such a relatively short time? How could they take over the possessions of the United States in the Pacific so easily? The answer is simple. The United States had no fortifications on its islands to stop the Japanese aggression, and the reason we did not have any fortifications was because of the Pacific Demilitarization Agreement. The sad fact was that our policies of the 1920s spun us tragically towards disaster in 1940.

Since most of the major powers of the world had delegates in Washington, D.C. for the disarmament conference, Secretary of State Hughes now used the time to hammer out two other agreements with foreign powers. He was able to get the United States, England, Japan, and France to agree that they should respect each other's rights and possessions in the Pacific. Furthermore, they agreed to refer any and all disputes which might arise in that region to a joint conference and to consult with each other in case there was a threat to peace in the Pacific from any outside power. This was known as the Four Power Treaty or Pact.

Next under Hughes' remarkable leadership was concluded what has become known in history as the Nine Power Pact or Treaty. In this treaty, Hughes was able to win official recognition of the United States' Open Door Policy in China, a policy which was first enunciated by the United States in 1899-1900. The Open Door Policy basically said (1) That all nations should respect Chinese territory rights and (2) that all nations should uphold the ideals of fair competition in China. In 1922 nine other nations signed an agreement to go along with the United States on this idea. Besides the United States, Japan, England, France, China, Italy, Belgium, Holland, and Portugal all agreed that they would respect the sovereignty and territorial integrity of China and that they would refrain from taking advantages of China's weak condition to seek some special commercial rights or privileges for themselves. It was interesting to note, however, that the treaty did not commit its signers to any kind of action if one of them violated the agreement.

Now that all these treaties had been signed, sealed, and delivered, America felt she had done her part to prevent another World War. Secretary of State Hughes, it has been said, with the stroke of a pen sank more ships than any admiral in history. As far as the United States was concerned it felt that world peace could be achieved and maintained by self-denying ordinances whereby each nation would pledge its honor to uphold each agreement. The United States sought to prevent another war by limiting

28

arms and signing pledges of nonaggression and if any power of the world did break the peace, the mobilization of world public opinion, it was felt, would force that country which had violated the agreements and the peace to reevaluate its position.

With Harding's death Calvin Coolidge became the next president of the United States and it was during his administration that the Harding scandals broke loose. None of the dirt that was turned up could touch Coolidge as he was the symbol of pristine virtue.

He was born on a farm in Vermont which had been cut out of the wilderness by his forebearers and which had been worked by the Coolidge family for five generations. As he grew up, he came to love the green hills and the stony earth of Vermont and built up a dislike for cities and a distrust for city people as he felt they were slickers living in citadels of sin. He went to a one-room schoolhouse in Plymouth and after school and on weekends he did chores around the farm like splitting wood, milking cows, feeding the chickens and hogs, and plowing the fields behind a team of horses. Furthermore, he was raised in the magnificent tradition of New England's town hall government, probably the most successful form of democracy ever practiced.

As for his looks, he was a meager looking man with a hatchet-pinched type face. In fact it led some people to comment that he looked as if he had been weaned on a pickle as he wore an expression on his face which made him appear like a person looking down his nose to locate some evil smell which forever seemed to be in front of him. He was a pale, stand-offish person with a closed mouth and was as silent as a wall as he did not believe in spending words in idle pleasantries. Words with Calvin Coolidge were not a free medium of exchange. They were a rare and precious commodity not to be wasted. Even his biographers noted this and one said Coolidge spoke so rarely that when he did open his mouth, a moth would fly out of it.

Calvin Coolidge began his political career in Massachusetts in 1898 and within twenty years he rose from the State Legislature to become the Governor of the State. Then in 1920, to balance the Republican ticket, he was selected to run for the vice-presidency. When the Harding-Coolidge ticket won the election of 1920, the Coolidges moved to Washington, D.C. and lived at the Willard Hotel. When he and his wife were invited out to dinner, Calvin would readily accept all the invitations. He would always enjoy his meal, and sometimes he would sit through an entire evening without saying a word. A sympathetic woman who saw that he dined out almost every night, asked why he did so . . . was it in the interest of the Republican party that he had to accept these dinner invitations all the time? Coolidge, as you know did not waste words and simply replied . . . "Got to eat somewhere." On another occasion a young lady at a dinner party asked to be seated next to the Vice-President. Once seated next to him she said, "Mr. Vice-President, I've made a rather sizeable bet with my friends that before the evening is over, I can get you to say at least three words." Coolidge looked at her with that stern New England look of his and replied . . . "You lose." He never uttered another sound the rest of the evening. Calvin came by his silence naturally. When his father John Coolidge was interviewed by the press, one of the newsmen commented to him that his son didn't say very much. Mr. Coolidge replied . . . "He ain't gabby." And that was all he said.

Critics of Calvin Coolidge have said that where the Washington Monument pierces 585 feet into the sky to symbolize the greatness of George Washington's contributions to his country, Coolidge's monument should be a hole dug straight down into the ground with a railing around it to keep anybody from falling in. This monument would be to commemorate all the things that Calvin Coolidge failed to do for his country as he was utterly without imagination, without ideas, and would not be caught dead making policy. As his critics put it . . . He was about as expansive as a letter box.

Yet, as Calvin Coolidge was sworn into office as the 30th President of the United States by his father, who was a justice of the peace, he had a lot of things going for him. He was an incorruptible man as he made no promises, no bargains, and no deals. He did no man's bidding and maintained his self-respect so impregnably that he won the admiration of everyone who came in contact with him. He was the living symbol of Yankee frugality known and trusted in the remotest part of the United States. He loved routine jobs and would take pride and pleasure in the performance of the simplest duties. He was so economical that he would go down in history as the only president to save a small fortune out of his salary while in the White House. Furthermore, in the years of the 1920s when American society was changing at a frightening pace, many Americans sought security by trying to hold on to their older virtues and Calvin Coolidge seemed to be the most suitable symbol in the country whereby people could feel secure that things would not change too fast. The ceremony of his father's swearing him into the Presidency in the Vermont farmhouse in which he had been born and the reading from the family Bible by a kerosene lamp was eaten up by the American people. To the people of the United States, this seemed to be the best possible guarantee that Coolidge would be the antidote needed to

Calvin Coolidge at his inauguration as the 30th president of the United States.

correct the wrong doings of the Harding Administration. His up-bringing in Vermont summoned up images for the American public of virtue in democracy like that of the honesty and sincerity of a New England town meeting.

Coolidge came along when the country was in need of moral bolstering. He was the embodiment of old maxims which almost everyone had forgotten. He himself was an image of the Horatio Alger story which was the story of . . . poor boy makes good. Coolidge believed that success which was made in any walk of life was measured almost exactly by the amount of hard work that was put into it. To the American people Calvin Coolidge suggested the rugged honesty of the New England hills, rural virtues, clean living, religious faith, and public propriety. His philosophy of life was so old that to many Americans it looked like something brand new. It was exactly what many Americans had been taught when they were little kids sitting on their mother's knee and it touched the pioneer spirit which was in the hearts of most Americans then and is still today.

As for his governing of the country, Coolidge felt that the business of America was the business of America and should not be interfered with by the government. He felt that if one did not try to interfere with the moral laws of the universe, which were good and enduring, everything would work out extremely well . . . so Calvin Coolidge did nothing to interfere.

It was during this period of time in the 1920s that there was also a revolution in morals. The disintegration of traditional American values was reflected so drastically in the change of manners and morals during this time that it shook American society to its foundations. People had lost their fear of hell and at the same time had less interest in heaven as now they made more demands for materialistic fulfillments here on earth.

The authority and the unity of the family had been gradually eroded away over the centuries with the rise of the cities. As the family lost its functions to the state, the factories, the schools, and to mass amusements, the chief test of the family by the 1920s was how well a family developed the personality of the children.

Then too, by the 1920s the moral code of the country was changing rapidly. To summarize this code (as it was viewed during the twenties) women were the guardians of morality. They were made of "finer stuff" than men and were expected to act accordingly. Young girls had to look forward to innocence and to a romantic love match which would lead them to the altar; whereby they would live happily ever after, and until the right man came along, they must not allow a male to kiss them. It was expected that some men would succumb to the temptations of sex but only with a special class of outlaw woman. Girls of respectable families were not supposed to have any such temptations. Boys and girls were permitted a large freedom to work and play together, but only under the watchful eye of a chaperone. The majority opinion held in the country was that it was wrong for women to smoke, and one could only imagine how shocked a person would be if a young lady took a drink of alcohol.

But now during the 1920s, boys and girls just growing out of adolescence were making mincemeat of this code.

The new woman wanted the same freedom of movement that men had and the same economic and political rights as well. Women began chanting slogans like . . . "Come out of the kitchen" and "Never darn a sock." Feminist leaders rebelled against the age old household roles of women and they were demanding more of marriage than they had ever demanded before. Not only that but their dress code went to new heights. In July of 1920, fashion writers were saying that the American woman had lifted her skirts far beyond any modest limitation. What they were saying was that women's skirts were now nine inches above the ground. The article went on to predict that after the fad had run its course, the hemline would begin to come down.

32

Band leader and comedian Ben Bernie, whose phrase, "Yowsah, Yowsah, Yowsah" is the title of this book!

But instead of that happening, the hem line climbed a few more scandalous inches higher, and some women were even abandoning their corsets.

If all this wasn't bad enough, the current mode of dancing created still more consternation. No longer did the romantic violins dominate the orchestra, now it was the barbaric saxophone. To the sax's passionate wailing, the fox trotters of the twenties danced so close together that not even an inch of space separated the couples. They danced as if they were glued together, body to body, cheek to cheek.

Morality groups began to cry out that the music was sensuous, that embracing partners and females only half dressed was absolutely unforgiveable conduct. Furthermore, the motions made by the dancers were suggestive! The forces of morality now rallied to the attacking of barbarism in this new age. Christian groups declared that the modern dances were indecent. Doing away with the Victorian dance forms like the waltz and yielding to the fast-stepping Charleston, the Black Bottom, and the slow sexy fox trots was an offense against the purity of women and was debasing the very fountainhead of the family and civilized life. The new styles of dancing were impure, polluting, corrupting, debasing, destroying spirituality, and increasing carnality. Youth was warned that the work of the devil and his followers was carrying the present and the future generations closer to chaos and destruction.

Indeed! The age of the Flapper had arrived. The Flapper? According to F. Scott Fitzgerald, the ideal flapper was a lovely young thing about 17-19 years of age who was bent on playing down her feminity and emphasizing her boyishness. She had bobbed her hair and dyed it raven black. She concealed everything feminine but her legs. She wore a tight felt hat, two strings of beads, bangles on her wrists, flesh-colored stockings rolled below the knees, and painted her face by dabbing her cheeks with two circles of rouge, and her lips with kissproof lipstick. In short, the flapper was the beginning of the American Youth Cult. Be Young, Stay Young, and Never Grow Old.

Meanwhile, to make matters worse, innumerable families were torn with dissension over cigarette smoking. For years smoking had been something only males could and well . . . nice girls just didn't smoke. If a girl did smoke, she was considered a brazen lady of the street. Liggett & Meyer, makers of Chesterfield cigarettes now decided to try and change all of that and make it socially acceptable for women to smoke in public if they wanted. But to do this, they would have to change the social mores of the country. To this end they hired an advertising executive by the name of Albert Lasker and told him that he had an unlimited budget with which to work. Lasker had his work cut out for him. Why just 20 years earlier, a group of daring women protesting the Victorian standards to which they were being held, smoked on 5th Avenue in New York City. They were promptly arrested and taken before a magistrate who fined them for being hussies.

Lasker began his campaign by using the radio, newspapers and magazines to reach the public. On the radio you would hear a sexy voice say *"Blow Some My Way."* This of course referred to the fact that a young lady in the company of a young man who was smoking a cigarette, wanted her male companion to blow some of the smoke her way so she could enjoy the aroma of the cigarette. Magazine and newspaper advertisements would show a young lady sitting on a moonlit beach with her escort who was lighting a cigarette. The only words in the picture were "Blow Some My Way." It took Lasker four years to move the female closer and closer to that cigarette, but finally he took his last and most dangerous step when a young lady was shown smoking a cigarette. The ad said, "Smoke Chesterfields, They Satisfy."

The 1920s also saw a revolution in manners and morals. Parents would lie awake nights waiting for their sons and daughters to come in from what were called all-night automobile rides, where heavy petting went on. The situation which brought on this revolution in manners and morals was World War I. Everyone in the country was affected in some way or other by the great war which had just taken place and an eat-drink-and-be-merry-for-to-morrow-we-die spirit seemed to develop in the country. The younger generation of the 1920s now refused to settle down into a humdrum routine of life as if nothing ever happened. They refused to accept the moral dictates of their elders, who they felt were living in a Pollyanna land, and whose rosy ideals were killed in World War I.

Furthermore, the new way of life of the 1920s was accelerated by the growing independence of American women. After the passage of the Nineteenth Amendment, women wanted to be freed from the drudgeries of housekeeping. They learned how to make lighter work out of preparing meals. The sales of canned foods grew and the number of delicatessen stores throughout the country increased three times. Bakeries increased their production as much as 60 percent and home made bread became a memory which was tucked away in the history books. Housewives also bought ready made clothes at the stores and spared themselves the rigors of dressmaking.

But the big thing that set the new generation free was Sigmund Freud. Before World War I Freud's name was known only by a few medical critics and a coterie of intellectuals. Freud had published a book on psychoanalysis at the turn of the century and after World War I this Freudian gospel began to circulate and extend itself to the American public. "According to Freud" (most conversations would begin), sex was the central, driving force which moved mankind and civilization. Almost every human motive Freud at-

Dr. Sigmund Freud of Vienna, is shown in above photo about to embark on his first airplane flight.

tributed to sex. If you were patriotic or liked the violin you were in the grip of sex in some sublimated form. And according to the interpretations of Freud, the first requirement of mental health was to have an uninhibited sex life. If you were to be well and happy, you must obey your libido. And as the Freudian doctrines made their way through the 1920s, people bandied about a new lexicon of words like: inferiority complex, sadism, masochism, and Oedipus complex. If you were a rich person you could go to Europe to be analyzed. If you were a working person you would have to settle for the analysts who plied their new trade here in the United States.

The American clergy in the meantime preached out against Freudianism by saying what was needed was virtue and self-control. Their words however were not even heard, as the American public yawned and looked down its nose at self-control which they felt was something that was out of date. According to the current Freudian thought, unless you freely expressed your libido and gave outlet to your sex energies, you could seriously damage your health.

Add to all of this the enormous increase of the use of the closed auto-

36

mobile and you now had a means of escaping temporarily from the supervision of parents, chaperones and from the influence of the prying eyes of neighbors. By jumping into a vehicle without asking anyone's permission, the closed car in effect became a room protected from the weather which could be occupied at any time, day or night and could be moved at will into a darkened byway or country lane and lend itself to the Freudian outlet between young couples.

All of this behavior and thinking next brought on a bumper crop of sex and confession magazines and lurid motion pictures. These in turn had their effect on the readers and movie-goers who would have never even heard of Freud and the libido.

Actress Theda Bara.

The movies drew millions of people to their doors everyday and they played to the same lucrative theme. Producers advertised that their pictures had sex symbols and jazz babies. When Theda Bara appeared in the "Blue Flame," she was called "The Vamp." Crowds mobbed theaters to get in. Then there was the *It* girl Clara Bow, and no one had to be told what *It* was. Hollywood played up the ideas of sex along with champagne baths, midnight revelries, and petting parties until dawn.

37

All of this influenced the younger generation. Girls who went out on dates now petted and when they did not pet they necked. No one was quite certain what the difference exactly was.

By 1924, manufacturers were deluged with complaints from retailers that skirts would have to be shorter. Shorter they were made and then still shorter. The knee-length dress proved to be exactly what women wanted. All of this meant that other changes in the weight and material in women's clothing would have to be made. Silk or rayon stockings and underwear supplanted cotton. Flesh colored stockings became the standard, and the long skirt and petticoat almost vanished from the American scene. Women were indeed shedding one layer of clothing after another. But women were not just content with their new clothing styles, they also showed their freedom by having their hair cut short as the bobbed head became the new style.

The manufacturers of cosmetics and the proprietors of beauty shops also did a landslide business. The vogue of rouge and lipstick hit with a bang. In the early 1920s, parents were alarmed with the younger generation using such things, yet by the midtwenties the vogue had spread to the remotest town in the country. Women who would have earlier thought that the use of paint was immoral were soon applying it regularly as a matter of course and making no effort to disguise the fact. Beauty shops sprang up on every street to give facials, to apply pomade, to make war against the wrinkles and sagging chins of age. They would pluck and trim and color the eyebrows and all of this was done to enhance and restore the bloom of youth. The youth cult began and it seems that the idea of growing old in the United States was a thing of the past.

The late afternoon cocktail party also became a new institution in America even though there was prohibition in the country. Women who a few years before would have gasped at the thought that they would drink alcohol, now found themselves in this new age matching the men drink for drink and enjoying the uproarious release caused by the spirits.

Indeed! Modesty, reticence, and chivalry were old hat and going out of style. Victorianism and Puritanism were becoming terms of abuse. It was insulting and near infamy to refer to some as Victorian or Puritanical. Up-to-date people thought of Victorians as old ladies with bustles and inhibitions; and of puritans as blue-nosed, ranting spoil sports. It was better to be modern, for to be modern was considered to be sophisticated and smart. And to show you were sophisticated and smart, the "in" thing to do was to smash the conventions of old. One should no longer be coy about things but be devastatingly frank.

Everyone wanted to be unshockable. And it was delightful to be considered a little shocking. So on came the boldness of talk and the use of words like "damn" and "hell." Soon, they became commonplace in everyday talk. There is no doubt that this revolution in morals during the twenties routed out the worst of the Victorian sentimentality and false modesty. Yet there were millions of people who became disillusioned without the old morality, as they could not endure a life without values and the only values they had been trained to understand were now being undermined. To many people during the 1920s everything seemed meaningless and unimportant. But at least they could toss down a few drinks and forget that their old world had crumbled. By the end of the 1920s however, a new moral code had taken over from the Victorian Age as people knew that in order to live in this new world and to live with themselves, they must have a moral code to guide them. And from the ruins of the old moral code, some of the enduring standards which could never be replaced were incorporated into the new code.

It was also during the early 1920s that the violent white supremacist organization known as the Ku Klux Klan reached its peak. The story of the rebirth of the 20th century Klan opens officially in 1915 but its history stems back to a day in 1901. On a fine Sunday afternoon in that year "Colonel" William Joseph Simmons, a southern preacher, while sitting on his front porch gazed into the sky. There he watched the wind drive masses of cumulus clouds along. Then all of a sudden he saw the clouds make an interesting formation; a formation of the Cross. Simmons took this phenomenon as a sign from God, fell to his knees and began praying. Simmons, who was an ex-veteran of the Civil War and a devotee to Southern history, felt that this was a sign for him to bring back the old Ku Klux Klan which had originally been founded in 1866 in Pulaski, Tennessee.

It was in 1866 that a group of young ex-Confederate officers started the Klan. The fact was that the Klan was nothing more than a social club of ex-veterans. They chose for themselves the name Kuklos, a greek word which means circle. Eventually the word Kuklos was separated and changed to Ku Klux and Klan was added to show unity. Later on the 1866 Klan degenerated into a terrorist group of southerners which dispatched Carpetbaggers, Scalawags and Blacks from southern offices and once white supremacy was restored to the south, the Klan was disbanded.

It was not until 1915 that Simmons felt he was prepared to launch his great task of re-awakening the Klan. On Thanksgiving Night of 1915, he led a troop of 16 followers up Stone Mountain, Georgia (near Atlanta) and there at midnight he lighted a fiery cross to call forth the Invisible Empire from its slumber of a half century.

The new Klan operated in secrecy. It had a Kloran which was its book of rules and rituals. To become a Klansman one had to be a native born, white, gentile American, who was free from any allegiance to any government, cause, people, sect, or ruler that was foreign to the United States of America. He must believe in the tenets of the Christian religion, take a solemn oath to defend, preserve, and enforce the Constitution; be faithful to fellow Klansmen and strive for the eternal maintenance of white supremacy.

Then too, the Kloran had a secret language for Klansmen to use in what were called Klonversations. The code was based on an exchange of the first letters of words in a sentence. For instance: Let us say you met another person and you wanted to ask him "ARE YOU A KLANSMAN?" The "A" from the word ARE, the "Y" from the word YOU, the "A" from A and the "K" from the word KLANSMAN were all put together to make up a word . . . A-Y-A-K. The reply to AYAK if you were a fellow Klansman would be AKIA . . . "A Klansman I Am." KIGY would follow next. K-I-G-Y meant "Klansman, I greet you." Then the two Klansmen would clasp left hands which was the sign of the Klan loyalty and sacred purpose. If when a Klonversation was taking place between the two Klansmen, a non-member approached, the Klansman who spied him first would break off the Klonversation with a sarning: SAN-BOG" . . . which meant . . . "Strangers are near be on guard."

Parade of the Ku Klux Klan, past the Treasury Building in Washington, D.C., 1925.

40

Nonmembers of the Klan were aliens and remained that way until they were baptized as citizens of the Invisible Empire. Once a nonmember was baptized, he had to take an oath which informed him that if he kept his oath it would mean honor, happiness, and life; but if the new member violated his oath, it would mean disgrace, dishonor, and death. Furthermore, the member also swore absolute obedience to the Imperial Wizard, who was described in the Kloran as "The Emperor of the Invisible Empire, a wise man, who was a wonder worker and had the power to charm and control."

Simmons now went about trying to enroll people in his newly established Invisible Empire. By 1920 he had enlisted fewer than three thousand people. Then he happened to run into a couple of professional fund raiser and publicity agents, Mr. Edward Young Clarke and Mrs. Elizabeth Tyler, who were the owners of the Southern Publicity Association. They were big timers and had raised millions for the Anti-Saloon League and the Roosevelt Memorial Fund. The Ku Klux Klan was almost too small to be worth their attention, but the two fund raisers decided that it had real possibilities for growth if handled right.

They saw that an organization like the Ku Klux Klan had an appeal to racial and religious hatreds and had a driving force that could be put on a businesslike, paying basis. Yes Sir! There were endless possibilities.

They joined the Klan and talked Simmons into letting them handle the promotion. Simmons agreed and the two sat down and went to work. They divided the country into eight domains. Each domain was to be headed by a Grand Goblin. Then the domains were subdivided into realms which were usually states and each realm was headed by a Grand Dragon.

To get into the Klan called for an initiation fee of $10. Four of the ten dollars went to the Kleagle (the local member who had signed up the new recruit), one dollar went to the state level office of the Klan, fifty cents went to the Grand Goblin who headed the domain and the other four dollars and fifty cents went to the national headquarters of the Klan in Atlanta, Georgia. Robes which were made by the Gate City Manufacturing Company in Atlanta were sold to members for six dollars and fifty cents each. They cost three dollars and twenty-eight cents to make, so you can see the profit that the National Klan made from each member it brought in. Furthermore, additional money was made from the sale of the Klan's handbook, newspapers, and magazines which were printed by the Search Light Publishing Company in Atlanta. Not only that, but local Klaverns were supported by dues of one dollar per month.

In less than six months after Mr. Clarke and Mrs. Tyler started their

41

drive to enlist members into the Klan, they had passed well over the 100,000 mark. And between 1920-1925 the Klan grew to between four and five million members. Blazing crosses, the symbol of the Invisible Empire, were burned in every part of the country.

What caused the Klan to grow so swiftly? The facts seem to be that Clarke and Tyler exploited the fears and prejudices of many Americans of that day and age. They saw to it that the Klan provided a hate for every need and for every person. Besides the Blacks, Jews, Orientals, Catholics, aliens, bootleggers, violators of the Sabbath, night club and roadhouse owners were also put on the Klan's hate list. But why should this have been possible in a country which calls itself the melting pot of nations? The answer seems to be that World War I and the massive immigration to the United States which ensued thereafter were two important reasons. Wartime hatred of Germans was now translated into peacetime suspicion of foreigners as older Americans feared that they would become a minority to all of these other groups.

The Klan preyed upon the deadly monotony of everyday life. With its mystery, its parades at night illuminated by burning torches and crosses, by filling the air with unearthly incantations and secrecy, the Klan gave the person who joined a sense of belonging. It made small people feel important. And as always, the uninformed and unthinking American became the most dangerous person to his own democracy.

With its membership swollen to over four million persons, the power of the Klan became awesome. The Klan boycotted businessmen, used its influence to keep the United States from becoming a member of the League of Nations, and maimed hundreds of people in the name of law and order.

By 1922 a Doctor Evans (a dentist) who had become the Grand Dragon of the Realm of Texas worked his way up to become secretary of the national organization. From here it was just a hop-skip-and-a-jump to becoming the Imperial Wizard of the National Klan. This he did on Thanksgiving Day of 1923. Simmons, the organizer of the Klan, was out as Dr. Evans stole the show and the ex-emperor of the Klan was now a has-been. As for Colonel Simmons, he fought back by organizing a rival group to the Klan. They called themselves the Knights of the Flaming Sword. It fell flat. Then again in the 1930s, Simmons tried to form a new group. This time it was known as the White Band. This also had its beginnings in the post Civil War period and was a group of white vigilantes. But Simmons had no better luck with this than he did with the Knights of the Flaming Sword. In May of 1945, Colonel Simmons, founder of the 20th Century Ku Klux Klan died. He died broke and disillusioned.

With the Klan at its peak of power in 1924, and with 35,000 new members joining everyday, Dr. Evans, the Klan's new leader, decided to move the Klan into the realm of politics. Using their influence they kept Alfred E. Smith, a Catholic and the Democrat's strongest candidate, from getting the Democratic nomination in 1924. After many angry hours of meetings in smoke filled rooms, John W. Davis, a lawyer for J.P. Morgan and Company, was to win the 1924 Democratic nomination as a compromise candidate. Indeed, for Dr. Evans and his goblins and dragons, it was a very encouraging show of strength and the Klan looked forward to 1928.

Then all of a sudden, disaster struck the Klan. D.C. Stephenson, one of the highest ranking and most highly regarded men of the Klan committed a heinous error. He was considered to be the grandest dragon of the empire, and yet it would be he who would commit this error. Steve, as he was usually known, was a man who knew what he wanted. He wanted money, women and power. He even saw himself being President of the United States.

Steve was 33 years old, had a fleshy, handsome face and blond hair. He had thin eyebrows, a small mouth and small shrewd eyes. He was hearty and robust as a country drummer and was as cold as a hangman. He made his way up through the Klan by preaching righteousness and enlisting new members. He joined the Klan in 1920, became an organizer and by 1922 he succeeded in organizing the Klan in 20 different Midwestern states. By July 4, 1923, Steve officially became the Grand Dragon of Indiana and presided over their Konclave at Kokomo. Steve was a rising star in the Klan. Yet, Steve had a few hang-ups; he was vain, licentious, drank too much and was over-sexed.

His downfall came because of a woman by the name of Madge Oberholzer. She had a small job at the state capitol in the office of the State Superintendent of Public Instruction in Indiana. She was unmarried, 28 years old and not particularly attractive; which in Indiana meant she was ripe for spinsterhood. She was a buxom 145 pound individual, had a rather long nose and wore her hair in an exaggerated upsweep that hung over her forehead. For some reason Steve, whose tastes usually ran for ripe beauties, was interested in Madge. He took her to several parties and was seen everywhere with her.

On the night of March 15, 1925, Madge came home about 10:30 from dating another man. Steve had been telephoning all that evening. When he finally got her on the phone, he told her that he was going to Chicago and wanted her to come over. Steve sent Earl Gentry, one of his bodyguards, to escort her to his place. When she arrived she found Steve drinking and he forced her to drink with him. Three drinks later he asked her to go to Chicago with him. She refused. At that Steve motioned to Gentry and Earl Klenck, another bodyguard. They produced guns and the three men now led Madge outside to Steve's waiting car. They drove to the railroad station and boarded the midnight train for Chicago. There on the way to Chicago, Steve attacked Madge. He held her so she could not move and then raped her. So disgraced did Madge feel that she took six bichloride of mercury tablets. By the time Steve discovered what she had done she was deathly ill. He tried to get her to a hospital, he offered to marry her, and finally drove her back to Indianapolis. He took her to a loft over his garage and told her that he would keep her there until she agreed to marry him. She still refused and finally Steve had her taken home. There, several weeks later, Madge Oberholzer died. But before she died she dictated a full story of what had happened to her to the prosecuting attorney of Marion County, William H. Remy. A man who, by the way, was not controlled by the Klan.

The case caused an uproar across the nation as the press gave the trial of the Grand Dragon full coverage. The trial was moved to Noblesville, Indiana where Steve felt his Klansmen would acquit him of any wrong doing. He even went on to boast that he was the law. To his surprise, the Noblesville jury found him guilty of murder in the second degree and the judge sentenced him to life imprisonment. Then to Steve's further shock, Governor Ed Jackson, a man the Klan had helped elect, refused to pardon him. The case created such a bad smell that all of Steve's friends and political allies abandoned him. Steve by this time was desperate. He threatened to bring out a little black box which would embarrass the Klan and several elected officials in Indiana. He finally did produce his evidence with the hopes that this would get him off for turning states' evidence against the Klan for other things they had done. For a fact, the little black box and its contents did send a Congressman, the Mayor of Indianapolis, the Sheriff of Marion County, and other officials to jail. Even Governor Jackson was indicted, but the statute of limitations prevented him from going to jail.

Even though Steve had his revenge, he did not get his liberty. He tried every kind of threat and legal dodge, but all failed. The fact was that Grand Dragon Stephenson was a political prisoner.

Stephenson's crude mistake was a disaster for the Klan not only in Indiana but everywhere else as well. His trial was the sensation of the nation and his conviction was a national indictment of the Ku Klux Klan. After this incident, it became absurd and ludicrous for any member of the Klan to attempt to convert someone into becoming a member in the name of morality and the other good things for which the Klan supposedly stood, when the Klan's most powerful leader did the things Stephenson did and felt that he was above the law.

In one of the few photographs of him ever made, D. C. Stephenson is in the center conferring with his defense attorneys James Parker (left) and B.C. Jenkins (right).

The National Klan tried desperately to disassociate itself from Stephenson, but there was no way it could. Stephenson seemed to epitomize the man in the Klan and when he went down under a pile of rubbish, the Klan went too.

Almost as fast as the Klan grew, it died, although one might say that the Klan died hard for it was able to work its venon against Al Smith (a Catholic) who ran for the Presidency on the Democratic ticket in 1928. The Klan rallied what supporters it did have left around a battle cry "Keep the Pope out of the White House."

One of the crowning bits of irony in the story of the Ku Klux Klan happened in 1935 when the Klan's Imperial Palace in Atlanta, Georgia was purchased for $32,550 by the Catholic Church as a site for a new cathedral.

By 1944 all that was left of the Klan were a few local chapters with little or no appreciable strength in any states save Georgia and Mississippi.

Today, the Klan has less than 40,000 members and is all but a memory; a memory clouded with the passage of time, deserted, decadent, and overgrown by the brush of other events. Yet the Klan still exists and is just waiting in the wings of history to renew its strength on plain old fashioned ignorance. For when a new bogey man appears on the streets of America, the Klan will be ready to push forth with its venomous hatreds once more.

Chapter 3
THE FLIGHT OF THE *SPIRIT OF ST. LOUIS*

In this age of great space accomplishments, with men going to the moon and walking in space, in this age when space probes are going to Venus, it is hard to remember a time when man was earthbound, or when he was just learning how to fly. Yet such was the case, and it was not until the 1920s that man flew across the Atlantic Ocean. As daring and dangerous as it is for our astronauts today in space, that same element of danger and risk existed for every pilot who attempted to fly across the Atlantic Ocean from the American continent to Europe, as each pilot was completely on his own without the aid of computers or radio communication.

This journey into the past deals with one of the early pioneer flights of the Air Age, the flight of the Lone Eagle. This is the story of the flight of Charles Augustus Lindbergh, who flew from New York to Paris, by himself, in 1927.

Charles A. Lindbergh was born February 4, 1902. The first years of his life were spent on his father's farm near Little Falls, Minnesota. At an early age he displayed a remarkable mechanical aptitude, and by the time he was nine he knew as much about internal combustion engines as did local authorities. Throughout his high school career Lindbergh was rather shy. The only thing former classmates could remember about him was his daring recklessness on his motorcycle, which he acquired at about the age of fifteen. Before he graduated from high school, he was doing man's work on his father's farm. In September of 1920, Lindbergh enrolled at the University of Wisconsin as a mechanical engineering student. He neither smoked nor drank, as he believed these things were harmful to his body, and he even gave up coffee, as he believed that the caffeine reduced his steadiness of hand and eye.

In March of 1922, Lindbergh left school and went to Lincoln, Nebraska, where he enrolled as a flying student with the Nebraska Aircraft Corporation. The next May, after about eight hours of dual instruction, the school dissolved for financial reasons, and Lindbergh started barnstorming the country as a helper. As a helper, he would climb out onto the wing of a plane to attract the attention of townfolk over the town in which they were performing.

By the spring of 1926, Lindbergh started flying the Airmail planes between St. Louis, Missouri, and Maywood, Illinois. During his Airmail career he had to make four emergency jumps with a parachute, usually in bad weather when he couldn't find a flying field on which to land.

It was during the fall of 1926 that he thought out and laid the plans for his flight from New York to Paris. Way back in 1919, Raymond Ortiz, owner of the Brentwood and Lafayette Hotels in New York City, had offered $25,000 as a prize to the first pilot who would fly nonstop from New York City to Paris, France. Lindbergh made his plans for the Paris flight while still flying the Airmail. He decided that he would use a monoplane because he felt that it could carry a greater load at a higher speed. Because of the reliability of the up-to-date air-cooled radial engine, Lindbergh felt a single engine plane would be more efficient than a multi-engine plane. He felt a single engine monoplane would take him on a much longer flight, and would require much less fuel. Furthermore, the cruising range would be greater than that of a multi-engine craft.

About this time eight prominent men who lived in St. Louis, Missouri were looking for a pilot they could back for this adventure. They backed Lindbergh financially and gave him $15,000 to plan the flight. A few of the backers were Harry H. Knight, a broker and president of the State National

In this 1927 photo, Charles Lindbergh is shown with his plane, The Spirit of St. Louis.

Bank and the St. Louis Flying Club; Harold M. Bixby, president of the St. Louis Chamber of Commerce; and E. Lansing Ray, of the St. Louis Globe-Democrat newspaper.

In February of 1927, after several conferences in St. Louis and a couple of trips to New York City, an order was placed with the Ryan Aircraft Company of San Diego, California, who said they would build the required plane for $6,000 plus cost of instruments and engine. For the next two months the personnel of the Ryan corporation was caught in the spirit of the undertaking. Everyone was putting in overtime. Donald Hall, the chief engineer, recalled that he spent thirty-six consecutive hours over his drawing board. Lindbergh also lived in San Diego while the plane was being built. He used his knowledge and experience, along with Hall, to design the craft in which all emphasis was placed on range. Sharing Hall's office, Lindbergh carefully plotted his route. He thought of, and solved, every problem that could arise during his flight. Lindbergh's plane, the *Spirit of St. Louis*, was finished the last week of April. It was nine feet-eight inches high, twenty-seven feet-eight inches long, weighed 2,150 pounds empty, was designed to be 5,180 pounds fully loaded, and had a forty-six foot wingspan, ten feet more than the Ryan standard model. This would give more lift for the added weight of the extra fuel.

From April 28th to May 10th, flight tests were conducted around San Diego. Then on May 10th, Lindbergh gave the plane its first long distance flight. He flew to St. Louis from San Diego, California in fourteen hours and twenty-five minutes, which was the fastest trip from the coast to St. Louis ever made to that time. The next day he flew to New York City in a little over seven hours.

Upon landing his plane, Lindbergh found himself surrounded by reporters and cameramen. Lindbergh was also surprised to find all the men he planned on contacting out at the field waiting for him. A man from the Pioneer Instrument Company was there to install a new earth-inductor compass. The representative of the Vacuum Oil Company (which was handling his fuel), was there, and so were the builders of his new Wright J-5 Whirlwind engine. They were there to examine and overhaul that engine if it was necessary.

Other pilots planning to fly to Paris from New York City were at the airport at this same time. One was Commander Richard E. Byrd, who planned to fly to Paris in his plane called *The America*. There also, were Clarence Chamberlain and Bert Acosta, who were to pilot the craft built by Belonka called *The Columbia*. The question was, who would leave first, and of those who attempted the long flight, who would make it? Other men had tried to make this flight before, but all had failed. Many had crashed on take-off, while others flew off and went down in the ocean.

For about a week the plane was ready to go. Everything not absolutely necessary was sacrificed to decrease weight. Finally, on the afternoon of May 19, 1927, Lindbergh received indications that the weather was clearing over the Atlantic. He decided he would take off the next morning at daybreak, weather permitting. When he reached his room, he had two and a half hours to sleep. He knew sleep was important, but he couldn't sleep. There were just so many things he had to think about.

Roosevelt Field was picked for the take-off because it had the longest runway in the area. In the early morning of May 20th, the *Spirit of St. Louis* was towed to one end of the runway and filled with 450 gallons of gas. Because of the morning dampness, the engine didn't "rev-up" to its full capacity. Then the wind came. This meant that Lindbergh would have to take off with a five mile per hour tail wind on a soft runway. All eyes were on him as he sat in the cockpit. Only he could say yes or no. With a nod of his head, the mechanic pulled the blocks from under the wheel. The heavily overloaded plane started slowly. Then it gathered speed, and left those pushing it behind. Lindbergh had to stay on the narrow runway. The next question was, would he make it over the telephone wires at the end of the field? Should he stop while he could, or should he try to make it? These were the questions that raced through his mind. Four times the little plane rose, and again landed. Then, slowly it took off, over the fence, over the wires, then finally it cleared the trees.

Once he had cleared these obstacles he set his compass for the first one hundred mile segment of his Great Circle Route to Paris. Hundreds of papers all over America carried the story. Will Rogers wrote, "No attempts at jokes today. A slim, tall, bashful, smiling American boy is somewhere over the middle of the Atlantic Ocean, where no lone human being has ever ventured before." But the nations feeling of awe and mystery was perhaps best conveyed by Daniel R. Fitzpatrick in a drawing made for the *St. Louis Post-Dispatch*. The lower fourth of the cartoon showed an empty sea, the rest an immense gloomy sky, fretful of a storm. And in the center of that sky, poised in defiance, was a tiny plane.

By noon of the first day Lindbergh reached Nova Scotia. A check on navigation showed his error between Massachusetts and Nova Scotia was six miles, or two degrees off course. At sunset he flew over St. Johns, Newfoundland, which was his last checkpoint before Ireland. One must remember there was no automatic pilot or lock-on guidance system. Lindbergh had to fly it all the way. During the night he flew into a solid cloud wall. Suddenly he became aware that his wings were icing up rapidly. Slowly he turned around, hoping to reach clear air before the ice warped the wings and plunged him into the sea. For a moment, things were desperate. Then Lindbergh burst from the clouds, and the ice began falling off his wings. It was a close call, but he had made it, and thereafter he flew around the clouds. As the night dragged on slowly, Lindbergh spent his time trying to improve his navigation. But because of the ever-present longing for sleep, he found it hard to work with figures. How he continued to stay awake is all but a mystery.

As dawn broke on May 21st, he was still over the vast Atlantic. But then, on the 27th hour of his flight, Lindbergh's mind was reawakened when he spotted a small group of fishing boats on the horizon. He headed toward them, and swooping down low, he began to yell "Which way is Ireland'" "Which way is I reland?" He shouted as loud as he could but they didn't hear him. Receiving no reply, he headed his plane in the direction he thought Ireland was located. An hour later he was over Dingle Bay, Ireland, and he was two and a half hours ahead of schedule. The Irish immediately flashed the news to the rest of the world.

Lindbergh, in the meantime, had gotten his second wind. Refreshed, he flew over the English Channel and by sunset was over Cherbourg, France. He now flew over the farms of France heading toward Paris. Upon reaching Paris, he circled the Eiffel Tower and headed northeast to where he had been told LeBourget Field was located. After searching about, he found the airfield, where floodlights had been turned on to guide his landing. Slowly he brought his plane over the hangers, past the lights, and finally he touched down on the runway, and eventually rolled to a stop in the dark area beyond. There he was mobbed by cheering crowds.

Thus ended the first New York to Paris nonstop flight. Lindbergh had averaged over 107 miles per hour, covered the 3,610 miles in 33 hours and 29 minutes, and had broken the world's record for long distance nonstop flying. Lindbergh finally got to bed several hours later, after being rescued from the crowds that had engulfed him and his aeroplane at LeBourget Airport. He had gone 63 hours without sleep.

Every record for mass excitement and mass enthusiasm in this age of the 1920s was smashed during the next few weeks. Nothing seemed to matter, either to the newspapers or to the people who read them, but Lindbergh and his story. On the day the flight was completed, the *Washington Star* sold

16,000 extra copies, and the *New York Evening World* 114,000 extra copies. The huge headlines which described Lindbergh's triumphant progress from day to day in the newspapers from Maine to Oregon showed how the public was in complete agreement that Lindbergh had performed one of the greatest feats in the records of the human race.

After his flight, Lindbergh was received in Paris, Brussels, and London where he gave speeches before cheering crowds. President Coolidge ordered the United States cruiser, the *USS Memphis*, to London to bring him and his plane home. Upon his return to the United States he was greeted in Washington, D.C. at a vast open-air gathering at which the President made, according to many authorities, one of the longest and most impressive addresses that he had ever given. The Western Union provided message telegrams of congratulations to Lindbergh, and over 55,000 of them were sent.

His welcome in New York City was thunderous. After the public welcome in New York, the street cleaning department gathered up 18,000 tons of paper which had been torn up and thrown out of the office windows to make a snowstorm greeting. Lindbergh was commissioned a colonel and received the Distinguished Flying Cross, the Congressional Medal of Honor and so many foreign decorations and honorary memberships that to repeat the list would be a wearisome task. A Texas town was named after him, and a staggering number of streets, schools, restaurants, and corporations sought to share the glory of his name.

To appreciate how extraordinary this universal outpouring of admiration and love was, one must remind oneself of two or three facts. Lindbergh's flight was not the first crossing of the Atlantic by air. Adcock and Brown had flown direct from Newfoundland to Ireland in 1919. That same year the NC–4 with five men aboard it, had crossed the Atlantic by way of the Azores, and the British dirgible the R–34 had flown from Scotland to Long Island with 31 men aboard and then returned later to England in the same flight. The German dirgible, the ZR–3, later known as the *Los Angeles*, had flown from Frederickshaven, Germany to Lakehurst, New Jersey in 1924 with 32 people aboard. Furthermore, two American army planes had also crossed the North Atlantic by way of Ireland, Greenland, and Newfoundland in 1924. The novelty of Lindbergh's flight lay only in the fact that he went all the way from New York to Paris instead of jumping off from Newfoundland. Not only did he reach his precise objective, but he was alone.

Today, many years later, and long after Lindbergh's flight, as we sit back and take a critical look at things, we might well ask ourselves — Why?

Why this idolization of Charles Augustus Lindbergh? The explanations are varied, but it seems that the United States at this time was a disillusioned nation, fed up on cheap heroics, scandal and crime, and was spiritually starved. One by one the American people had seen their early ideas, illusions, and hopes worn away by the corrosive influence of events and ideas; by a disappointing aftermath of the war; by scientific doctrines and psychological theories which undermined their religion and ridiculed their sentimental notions; by a spectacle of graft in politics, crime on the city streets, and finally by the recent newspaper diet of smut and murder. Romance, chivalry, and self-dedication had all been debunked. The heroes of history had been shown to have feet of clay, and the saints of history had been revealed as people with strange complexes. There was a god of business to worship now, but a suspicion lingered that he was only made of brass. The public had been given contemporary heroes to bow down to before, but these contemporary heroes, with their fat profits from motion picture contracts and ghost-written syndicated articles, were not wholly convincing.

Something that people needed, if they were to live at peace with themselves and the world, was missing from their lives. All at once Lindbergh provided that need. Romance, chivalry, self-dedication, belief — here they were embodied in a modern Galahad for a generation which had forsaken Galahads. Lindbergh did not accept motion picture offers. He did not sell testimonials. He did not boast. He did not get himself involved in scandals. What he did do was to conduct himself with unerring taste.

And so we leave the past and return to our time. Do we see the same thing? Do we see people debunking our religions as useless institutions of an unenlightened generation which they consider superstitious fools? Do we find people dragging down our government, telling us it is a piece of tyrannical machinery designed to create myths and laws so that a few can use the majority as tools? Do we find those who do not want their rights denied them willing to deprive others of those same rights? The answer to all the questions, I'm afraid, is — yes.

Where is the Lindbergh of our time to lift up our spirits in these hours of chaos and confusion? Who is he? The Lindbergh of our time is you. You, who believe that the spirit of love and affection will triumph over distrust, falsehood, halftruths, lies and smut. It is you who believe in the life of self-dedication, chivalry and right. You are the heroes of our time.

Chapter 4

AND WHAT ELSE HAPPENED
DURING THE TWENTIES?

By 1924, there were over 2½ million radio sets in homes throughout the country, and it was in that year Americans for the first time heard their first political conventions drone on and on via the radio. The Democrats nominated John W. Davis after 102 hectic ballots and the Republicans nominated "Silent" Calvin Coolidge. In the November elections, Coolidge was elected to four more years in office on the campaign slogan "Keep Cool with Coolidge."

With the elections out of the way, Americans, who by now seemed numb to just about everything, were stunned by the story of the thrill killing of Bobby Franks by Nathan Leopold and Richard Loeb. Loeb, at the age of eighteen, was the youngest graduate in the University of Michigan's history and Leopold, nineteen, was Phi Beta Kappa and had a Bachelor of Science degree from the University of Chicago. Both were *Cum Laude* graduates and both were from well-to-do homes.

One afternoon in the spring of 1924 (after seven months of planning), they decided to kill a person just to see what it felt like. Then after they had killed their victim, they would dispose of the body, and get away with what they felt would be the perfect crime. They had no particular victim in mind until a neighbor by the name of Bobby Franks walked by. Bobby knew and liked Leopold and Loeb, and when the two boys offered the fourteen year old youngster a ride home from school, he eagerly got into their car. Bobby was taken about four blocks from his home. Then, all of a sudden, Loeb grabbed him and stuffed a gag into his mouth while at the same time Leopold took a heavy cold chisel and smashed it into his skull four times. With his skull split open, the young victim slumped into unconsciousness and died.

Leopold and Loeb next drove idly around Chicago until they came to a marshy wasteland outside the city. There they carried the still warm body over to the marsh and both took turns holding Bobby Frank's mutilated head under the swamp water until they were sure all life was gone from the boy's body. Next, they poured hydrochioric acid on the face of the youngster to make his identification more difficult, and wedged his body into a near-by drain pipe which was obscured by shrubbery and weeds.

Their "perfect crime" completed, the two murderers went to a restaurant and got something to eat. That night at Leopold's house they called Mr. Franks, a retired pawnbroker, and told him that the boy had been kidnapped and would be returned for $10,000. They went on to say that he would receive further instructions by mail on when and where to pay the ransom money. Mr. Franks notified the police immediately.

Then as fate would have it, two construction workers, taking a shortcut home through the marshy area outside of Chicago, found the body of the murdered boy. At first Mr. Franks would not believe the police when they told him they had found his son murdered, but eventually he accepted the fact that his son had been killed and his kidnappers were now asking for money for their infamous deed.

As the police moved in the case, they began to find clue after clue to this so-called "perfect crime." When they were disposing of the corpse, Leopold dropped his glasses, leaving them behind at the scene of the crime. It took the police eight days to trace down the oculist who made this prescription and from the evidence he gave them, Leopold was arrested.

Counsel for the Defense at the sensational murder trial of Leopold and Loeb. Left to right: Walter Bachrach, Clarence Darrow, Nathan Leopold, Jr., Richard Loeb (partly hidden behind Benjamin Bachrach). Walter and Benjamin Bachrach assisted Mr. Darrow in the defense.

Leopold protested he was innocent and came up with an alibi. He said he was out joyriding in his car with his friend Loeb, and Loeb backed his story. But the Leopold's chauffeur told police that Nathan's Willis-Knight car had never left the garage on May 21st. Then two newspaper reporters found Leopold's Underwood portable typewriter in a lagoon and the type matched the ransom note Bobby Frank's father had received. Under questioning, Loeb broke and confessed everything.

The trial which followed was the sensation of the country. Famed criminal lawyer Clarence Darrow was hired to defend the accused murderers. Darrow was able to convince the court that what these boys needed was a life time to think over the immensity of their crime. Judge John Caverly who heard the case without a jury (as requested by Darrow) agreed and both men were sentenced to life in prison without hope of parole.

Loeb was killed in a prison riot twelve years later in 1936, and Leopold lived long enough to finally be parolled in 1958. He devoted the rest of his life to serving humanity and died in Puerto Rico on August 29th, 1971.

By 1925 Americans became used to crime, as they saw it spring up almost everywhere because of the Prohibition Amendment. Writers and critics alike referred to the amendment as the "Noble Experiment." It went into effect on January 16th, 1920 and then the country settled back into a "Well, that's that" attitude. The Eighteenth Amendment in a sense was not only a protest against "Demon Rum," but it was also a defense by old rural America against the threat of industrialism and social change. From the earliest colonial times, farmers and frontiersmen viewed cities as the stronghold of Satan and the seedbed of every real and imaginary vice. It was in 1919, that the "Drys" (the people who supported prohibition and were against the consumption of alcoholic beverages) had secured ratification of the Eighteenth Amendment; and Billy Sunday, an evangelical preacher, said "Goodbye John Barleycorn, you were God's worst enemy and hell's best friend. Your reign of tears and misery are over."

The blissful, bone-dry utopia which the prohibitionists foresaw failed to arrive. Instead of utopia, there now flourished a horde of bootleggers, moonshiners, racketeers, venal judges, corrupt police and crooked politicians. Working together, this unholy crew took in billions of dollars by selling their illegal "hooch" to an eager and thirsty public. There were no prophets who could have foretold the awful things which would happen because of the new amendment. No one foresaw the rum ships prowling off the coasts, the illicit breweries and distilleries, the speakeasies, the corruption of the police and judiciary, the hijackers and their machine gun gang wars, the multimillionaire booze barons, the murders and assassinations, the breakdown of morals and manners, the rise of organized crime and the long train of evils which were to spring forth. Nor did anyone have any idea of how difficult it would be to enforce the law.

According to Thornstein Veblen, an economist of the times, drinking during the "Roaring Twenties" became a sign of superior status for those who were able to afford the indulgence. Women who previously would have never ventured into a saloon now drank and used drinking to show they were emancipated.

To accommodate the drinkers, over 220,000 illegal saloons known as speakeasies sprang up. In one of the big city speaks Texas Guinan welcomed her customers by yelling out "Hello, Suckers!" She cleared up to $4,000 per week by providing customers with exotic settings, songs and skits. Texas always insisted that she didn't sell the stuff because her customers brought their own booze in their hip flasks. The truth was, however, that you could get a booster when your flask ran dry if you knew the headwaiter, or if you looked like you knew him, or if you knew somebody who was pretty sure he knew him, or maybe you could get a drink if you were thirsty and didn't look like one of those seedy prohibition agents.

At Belle Livingston's joint customers were required to sit on the floor in oriental style because as Belle put it, "A person could get hurt falling off a bar stool." After torch singer Helen Morgan's place was raided for serving booze, she was placed on trial. The jury quickly dismissed the case by saying that they could not take the word of the two prohibition agents against the word of Miss Morgan that she was selling liquor.

But not all the joints were as classy as Texas Guinan's, Belle Livingston's, or Helen Morgan's. By contrast, there were some places called "Smoke Joints" where they sold wood alcohol and Jamaica ginger which blinded, paralyzed or killed thousands of Americans by the end of the Era of Prohibition. But to most Americans those things happened to the other fellow, not them.

To enforce the Eighteenth Amendment, only 1,500 prohibition agents were hired by the federal government. These noble snoopers were paid an average of about $2,500 per year and were supposed to keep 125,000,000 people honest. The prohibition agents did their best, and two of them made a spectacular try to keep the nation dry. They were Isadore Einstein (Izzie) and Moe Smith. Their antics in rounding up law breakers were some of the most hilarious capers of the day and became a legend during the twenties.

Izzie lived on New York's Lower Eastside in a small $14 a month flat on Ridge Street. He was a bulbous little man who had been a salesman but was now a clerk for the post office. With a wife and four children to support, Izzie was looking for a better paying job. One day as he was reading the paper he read about the government's plan to hire agents to enforce the Eighteenth Amendment and that their salary would be about $2,500 per year.

So Izzie applied and was told by the chief enforcement agent in New York, James Shevlin, that he just didn't look the part. Mr. Shevlin was right, for Izzie was forty years old, almost bald, five feet-five inches tall and weighed about 225 pounds . . . most of it around his middle. Izzie wouldn't take no for an answer, however. He told his future boss that that was exactly why he should have the job because no one would ever suspect him of being a prohibition agent. Furthermore, he spoke Yiddish, German, Polish, and Hungarian fluently. Then too, he could make his way through French, Italian, Russian, and even knew a few words of Chinese. Mr. Shevlin shook his head and hired Izzie.

Izzie's first assignment was to clean up a place in Brooklyn. Authorities suspected the house to be a speakeasy since drunken men were routinely seen staggering from the building. Not only that, but the air for half a block around was reeking with fumes of beer and whiskey. Despite this, none of the agents had been able to get inside the place. Izzie knew nothing of sleuthing procedures. He simply walked up to the joint and knocked at the door. A peephole opened and a hoarse voice yelled out "Who's there?"

Izzie replied that he was Izzie Einstein and that he wanted a drink.

"Oh yeah? Who sent you here?" the voice inquired.

"My boss sent me," said Izzie. "I'm a prohibition agent and I just got appointed."

As the door swung open, the doorman slapped Izzie on the back, bid him to come in and while laughing his head off, told Izzie that was the best gag he'd ever heard.

There were half a dozen men drinking at a small makeshift bar as Izzie stepped in. The doorman was still laughing as he yelled to his boss, "Serve this man a drink, he's a prohibition agent." By this time everyone in the place was laughing, even the bartender. As Izzie stood there, the bartender asked him if he had a badge to prove that he was a prohibition agent. Izzie produced his badge and everyone laughed some more. As the bartender served Izzie, he commented on the fact that his badge looked just like the real thing. It was then and there Izzie informed everyone that they were under arrest. At that point, the joint exploded and the exit was jammed as people tried to escape.

Soon Izzie became the terror of the speakeasies. In many speaks his picture hung behind the bar so bartenders could identify him and destroy any evidence before it could be used against them.

Izzy Einstein and Moe Smith. The public loved and followed their antics. Would you suspect they were prohibition agents?

During the next five years, Izzie did all sorts of crazy things to arrest people who were violating the Eighteenth Amendment. Once he pranced into a gin-mill with his badge pinned to his lapel in plain sight and shouted, "Hey, how about a drink for a hard working prohibition agent?" Everyone who saw the jovial round little man trying so hard to be funny rushed forward and handed him a drink. Izzie took the drinks, arrested them and closed the joint.

Since Izzie was having the time of his life, he decided to share his fun with his close friend Moe Smith. Moe joined the force and was just like Izzie. He was a natural comedian, tipped the scales at about 235 pounds and was just as "roly-poly" as they come.

Newspapers during the 1920s were looking for stories with a connection to prohibition. Casting about for stories with humor, they seized upon the exploits of Izzie and Moe. The two fat agents would even schedule their raids to suit the convenience of the reporters. One Sunday, accompanied by a swarm of eager reporters, Izzie and Moe established a record by making seventy-one raids in little more than twelve hours.

Then there was the time that they staged a raid on a speakeasy for the Calvary Baptist Church. The entire congregation watched the agents bust the speak. While all of this was happening, the Reverend John Stratton, the pastor of the church, delivered one of his "hell-fire-and-damnation" sermons. After the sermon was over, the arrested persons were given a chance to repent as Izzie and Moe led them off to jail.

No morning newspaper during the early 1920s was complete without some story or account of the exploits of Izzie and Moe. What impressed everybody about the two men was their ingenuity. There was one New York speakeasy that agents could never quite nail down. So in came Izzie and Moe. On a cold winter night Izzie stood in front of the gin-mill in his shirt sleeves until he was red, shivering, and his teeth were chattering. Then Moe half-carried him into the speakeasy shouting excitedly, "Give this man a drink. He's just been frostbitten." The kindhearted bartender startled by Moe's excitement and upset by Izzie's miserable appearance rushed forward with a bottle of whiskey, which Moe promptly snatched, put the man under arrest and closed the place.

Then there was an exclusive Brooklyn club which catered to judges and lawyers only. The doorman to the club let Izzie in because he wore a frock coat and carried a huge law book under his arm. Once inside, Izzie opened the book, adjusted a pair of horn rimmed spectacles and as he was reading his book, he lifted his hand as a waiter went by and said, "A beverage please." When the drink was served, Izzie and Moe busted another joint.

One of the toughest places for Izzie and Moe to crack was an establishment that sold only soft drinks. The reason it became suspect was because its customers would come away tipsy after a few shots of soda water. It was a difficult joint to bust because the owner would never sell liquor to anyone he didn't know personally. For Izzie and Moe, it became a challenge. They got a group of agents, dressed them up in football uniforms, smeared them with fresh dirt and headed for the soda fountain. Izzie, with a football tucked under his arm, a helmut hung over his ears and his fellow agents whooping it up, moved into the speakeasy. There Izzie stated to the owner that they had just won the last game of the season and they now wanted to break training in a big way. The owner, pleased with such a rush of business sold each agent a pint of whiskey — and another speakeasy was busted.

60

Once Izzie received a letter from a distressed housewife stating that the man at the local grocery store charged her two dollars for a can of tomatoes. She went on to say that when she got home she found nothing in the can but a lot of nasty smelling water. When she told her husband, he grabbed the can, ran out of the house, and had not been seen since. Izzie naturally hustled down to the store and waited his turn in a long line of impatient customers. He discovered that in order to get whiskey, you ordered a can of beans. If you wanted gin, you asked for tomatoes. Izzie bought some of both and then busted the place.

For more than five years the whole country laughed at the antics of Izzie and Moe (with the exception of bootleggers and speakeasy proprietors). Then in 1925, some austere high official in Washington, D.C. who never got mentioned by the newspapers, put out a directive that agents were to keep their names out of the papers and that they were to act dignified at all times.

Within three months after the directive, Izzie and Moe were let go. They turned in their badges for what was called the "good of the service," and dropped out of the public eye save for an occasional Sunday feature story in a newspaper. Prohibition finally ended in 1933, with the passage of the Twenty-first Amendment which repealed the Eighteenth Amendment. With the end of prohibition, came the end of a somewhat colorful era of American history. Today names like Al Capone, Johnny Torrio, Dutch Schultz, and other hoodlums are all that most Americans remember about the noble experiment, but there are still enough people around who will always recall the colorful antics of Izzie and Moe.

Besides Izzie and Moe capturing the eye of the American public there were some other fads and fancy stuff for which Americans went wild. In the early months of 1923, a dried up little Frenchman by the name of Emile Coue arrived from France to go on a lecture tour. Suddenly he was the most talked about person in the United States. Institutes were established in his name, audiences thronged to hear the master speak and wherever he went, hushed audiences listened in awe as Emile Coue told them the secret of life.

Just who was Emile Coue and just why were crowds flocking to hear him? Coue was a short, thick-set man with grey hair and a goatee. He had a waxed mustache, penetrating brown eyes and a kindly smile. He walked with a slight stoop and dressed in a carelessly fitting black suit with a stiff white shirt and a black string tie.

Coue was born in Troyes, France in 1857. He became a pharmacist and did so well at pharmacy that in 1896 he retired from the business a wealthy man at the age of thirty-nine. Yet, four years later he came out of retirement and became involved with Dr. Liebeault. Dr. Liebeault taught his patients that most of their ailments were in their minds and through hypnotism made his patients feel better.

Coue found through his studies that Dr. Liebeault's patients recovered extremely well. It was then that Coue began to develop some theories of his own; that what a person wanted to be was what he thought he could be. Everyone, claimed Coue, was a puppet of his imagination and the only way people would cease to be puppets would be when they learned to guide their imaginations in the directions they wanted.

In order to guide your imagination, Coue went on to say, you must use what he called autosuggestion. If you wanted to be a better person, Coue suggested that every morning after you got up and every evening before you went to bed, you should look into a mirror and repeat out loud to yourself twenty times in succession . . . "Day by day in every way, I am getting better and better. Day by day in every way, I am getting better and better." Then with great faith, confidence and conviction, guess what would happen to that individual? He would get better and better because he believed in himself.

As a result of all of this, thousands of Americans flocked to hear Coue and then practiced what he preached. Even men of the clergy and medical doctors approved of it. Indeed, Emile Coue became the eternal voice of the fountain of optimism. And even today, Coue's idea still makes a lot of sense.

While everyone was reciting the verse that day by day in every way, he was getting better and better, another new craze started sweeping the country. It was a game called Mah Jong. Two brothers named White had introduced the game into the English-speaking clubs in Shanghai where it became very popular. Then it was brought to the United States and it won immediate favor. So much so that W.A. Hammond, a San Francisco merchant, began to import Mah Jong sets into the country on an ambitious scale. By September of 1922, he had sold over $50,000 worth of sets. Then he decided that perhaps an advertising campaign might help the popularity of the game so he advertised free lessons and exhibitions. This pushed the game quickly and by the time one year had gone by, Mah Jong had become a nation-wide craze. Chinese set makers could no longer keep up with the demand and American manufacturers started making the sets. Everywhere throughout the country people "broke the wall" and called out "pung" or "chow" and wielded the Ming box and talked learnedly about bamboos, flowers, seasons, one crack, south winds, east winds, and red dragons. The wealthy people bought $500 sets while the rest of the country purchased theirs for $5.95. Soon a Mah Jong League of America was formed. This brought on fierce debates as to what rules the game would be played by, what system of scoring would be used and what constituted a limited hand. Practically all "correct" dinner parties of the twenties ended with everyone setting up ivory and bamboo tiles on a green baize table to play Mah Jong.

Another craze to reach its peak in 1925 was the crossword-puzzle. Crossword-puzzles date back to at least 1913 and had been published by the *New York World* newspaper for years. But as it happened now, two young men who were launching their careers in the book publishing business, decided to publish a crossword-puzzle book. Big publishers felt that the book wouldn't sell, but Simon and Schuster felt it would. They were right and by April of 1925, the first edition of the crossword-puzzle book was sold out and a second edition had to be put to press to meet the public demand for this new fad.

The odd looking crossword-puzzle book with a pencil attached to it was a best seller and Simon and Schuster became publishers overnight. The craze swept everywhere and it was a dull newspaper which did not have a daily puzzle. Dictionary sales bounded upward. Women became crossword widows as their husbands paid more attention to finding out a four letter word meaning to jump high than they did to them (the word by the way is leap). Then too, there was the pastor in Pittsburgh who put the text of his sermon in the form of a crossword-puzzle. Trains carried dictionaries, and anybody you met on the street could tell you the two lettered name of the Egyptian sun god (whose name was Ra), or provide you with the two letter word which meant the opposite of down . . .

By late 1925, the crossword-puzzle craze began to die out and by 1926, contract bridge moved in to replace it. Yet, despite the decline of the craze, you will still see people today as they eat their morning breakfast or while riding a train to work, working out those crazy mind-boggling crossword-puzzles.

1925 also saw a new dance called the Charleston sweep the nation. It was originally introduced in cabarets but it spread throughout the country like no other dance of its time. The Charleston was a very active dance, featuring exuberant side kicks which contrasted sharply from the wiggling movements of the shimmy and other jazz dances of the early twenties. But because it was new, it was naturally condemned by moralists as an evil dance whose movements were provocative.

On the intellectual side of things, the National Spelling Bee was initiated by the *Louisville Courier Journal* and even today it is an event looked forward to by youngsters who wish to show off their spelling talents.

Next, from the top of the world, news arrived from Nome, Alaska that a diphtheria epidemic had broken out. In February, with the Bering Straits frozen over, the only way that an anti-diphtheria serum to combat the epidemic could be delivered would be by dog teams. From where the boat dropped off the serum to Nome would be a distance of 655 miles. A relay of dog teams to take the life saving serum to Nome was set up and the last lap of the journey was covered by a sled team driven by Cunnar Kasson. With his lead dog Balto, Kasson pushed on through a blinding blizzard in sub-zero weather to deliver the serum. He was half dead from the cold and nearly blinded by the blizzard by the time he got to Nome. The antitoxin stopped the epidemic and later on Kasson confessed that it was the dog Balto who made it through those last miles to Nome, and not him.

1925 also saw Vice-President Charles Gates Dawes settle the German War Reparation claims in Europe and establish a realistic way for all nations to pay off their World War 1 debt obligations. For his work in putting Europe's economy back on its feet (with what eventually became known as the Dawes Plan) and for alleviating the debt and inflationary miseries of Europe, Dawes was awarded the Nobel Peace Prize.

The human interest story of 1925, was the story of Floyd Collins. Collins was an obscure young Kentuckian who had been exploring an underground passage five miles from Mammoth Caves. His hope had been to find another cave which would attract tourists and from which he could make a little money by charging admission. As he was crawling out of the cave (about 125 feet from the top and daylight) a cave-in occurred which pinned his foot under a rock. So narrow and steep was the passage that those who tried to dig him out had to move along on their stomachs in cold slime and water. In the cave on their stomachs, rescue workers would pass back from hand to hand the earth and rocks they pried loose with hammers. Only a few people might have heard of Collins and the predicament he was in but for W.B. Miller, a young reporter for the *Louisville Courier Journal*. Miller wormed his way down into the treacherous passage and interviewed Collins. Then he became engrossed in the efforts to rescue him. Miller's vivid dispatches brought the entire nation alive to watch the struggle to rescue Collins.

When Miller had arrived at the cave he found only three men at the entrance warming themselves by a fire and wondering how to free Collins. Within a week, Miller's stories brought hundreds of people who would live in tents, milling crowds which had to be restrained by barbed wire barriers, and state troopers who kept order as the attempts to rescue Collins took place.

For eighteen days the nation held its breath as news reports came out of Kentucky as to the progress of rescuing Collins. Then came the news. Collins had died. The efforts of man to free one of their kind had failed. A genuine frustration seemed to grip the nation. But even before the mourning for Collins was over a new and (what seemed at the time) greater crisis arose in the United States. It was the trial of John Thomas Scopes at Dayton, Tennessee.

John Scopes was brought to trial at Dayton on May 5th, 1925 for teaching the doctrines of evolution in his classroom at Central High School. The Scopes case had great significance in that it dramatized one of the most momentous struggles of the age. That struggle was the conflict between religion and science; between a Modernist interpretation of the Bible and a Fundamentalist interpretation; and it also involved the question of the separation of Church and State. No trial of the 1920s was as controversial as was the Scopes case and it all got started because of the work of Charles Darwin.

John T. Scopes, whose trial did not end the controversy over the teaching of evolution in the schools.

In the 1850s, Charles Darwin, a British researcher, wrote a book called *The Origins of the Species*. In this book he stated that man may well have evolved from a lower form of animal. In 1884, Darwin's theory was popularized in the United States by a lecturer by the name of John Fiske.

The idea that man might have evolved from a lower form of animal caused an uproar in the country with people who took the Bible literally. For in the opening chapter of the Book of Genesis, it states that God created the heaven and earth, Adam and Eve and all of creation in six days. Darwin's theory seemed to state that it took millions of years for life to evolve and not just six days.

Two warring camps of thought now came into being. There were the fundamentalists who believed in the letter of the Bible and refused to accept any teachings whatsoever which seemed to be in conflict with the Good Book. The other group of people who seemed to be more liberal in their beliefs were called modernists. They tried to reconcile their beliefs with scientific thought, throw out what was outdated, retain what was intellectually sound and mediate between Christianity and those skeptical spirits of the age.

The position of the fundamentalists seemed almost hopeless. The tide of all rational thought in a rational age seemed to be running against them. But they were numerous and there was no doubt where they stood. They stood solidly against any doctrines which were contrary to what the Bible said.

The fundamentalists were especially strong in the south and in Tennessee, the state legislature passed a bill on March 13, 1925 which stated "It shall be unlawful for any teacher in any of the universities and all other public schools in the state to teach any theory that denies the story of the Divine Creation of man as taught in the Bible and to teach instead that man has descended from a lower order of animals."

Two men in Dayton, Tennessee now decided to test the new law. They decided they would break the law, force a trial by the courts and try to get the law declared unconstitutional. It was George Rapplyea, a mining engineer, along with John Scopes, a twenty-four year old teacher of biology at Central High School in Dayton, who decided to test the law. Fresh out of the University of Kentucky, Scopes would teach about evolution in his classes and then his friend Rapplyea would have him arrested.

The deed was done and shortly thereafter, Scopes was arrested and put on trial. Within little or no time at all newsmen sensed the potential of this story as they stated the case in headlines in newspapers across the country.

66

Sleepy little Dayton, Tennessee suddenly found itself on the map overnight. The public soon learned that the fight was to be a battle between fundamentalism on one hand and twentieth century modernism on the other.

Then the two real adversaries in this legal bout came to Dayton. The champions of both causes were headline personalities. To prosecute was William Jennings Bryan, three times an unsuccessful candidate for the Presidency of the United States on the Democratic ticket in 1896-1900 and 1908. Furthermore, he was Secretary of State under Woodrow Wilson and in his own right, a famous orator. Bryan told the press that his reason for being in Dayton was to bring this slimy thing called evolution out of the darkness. He felt that the facts of religion and evolution would at last meet in a duel to the death. Bryan considered himself an expert on the Bible and he was willing to defend the word of his God against any who would attempt to defile or defame it.

For Scopes' defense came the highly successful criminal lawyer Clarence Darrow who stated, "If today you can take a thing like evolution and make it a crime to teach in the public schools, then at the next session of the legislature you can ban books and newspapers. Next you can turn Catholic against Protestant and then you may turn Protestant against Protestant."

Next came gaunt Tennessee farmers and their families in mule drawn wagons and ramshackle Fords. They were quiet, godly people in overalls ready to defend their faith against any modernist, and yet, they were curious to know what this new fandangled evolutionary theory might be all about. Then too, the atmosphere of Dayton was not simply that of rural piety. No sir! Not by a long shot. There were hot dog and lemonade venders who set up stalls along the streets as if this was some kind of fair. Book sellers hawked volumes on biology. Over a hundred newspaper men poured into the town and Western Union installed twenty-two telegraph operators in the back rooms of corner grocery stores. Even in the courtroom, reporters and cameramen crowded alongside grim faced Tennesseans to get the best stories and pictures. Indeed, there was an air of suspense like that of an opening night at the theatre.

The trial opened with a pious prayer to which Darrow objected. Then the state presented evidence that Scopes taught in his classroom the fact that life had perhaps begun something like *600,000,000* years ago. This assertion in the courtroom brought gasps of disbelief from the audience.

It was a bitter trial and its climax came when the defense, which had been frustrated in every way, decided to call Bryan himself to take the stand as an expert on the Bible.

So great were the crowds and so hot was the temperature, that Judge Raulston moved the court out of doors to a platform which had been built against the courthouse under some maple trees. Benches were set out where the throngs listened as Bryan charged that the insidious doctrine of evolution would undermine the faith of the children of Tennessee, rob them of the chance to enter the Kingdom of Heaven and keep them from enjoying the bliss of eternal life. He further charged that Darrow had no other purpose for being at the trial than to slur at the Bible.

Clarence Darrow, left and William Jennings Bryan, silver-tongued defender of fundamentalism are shown above having a chat during the Scopes trial. The heat forced these opponents to doff their jackets.

Darrow, now in his shirt sleeves and galluses and with a Bible on his knee, objected to Bryan's statement and stated that he was there to examine Bryan on his fool beliefs of religion which no intelligent Christian on earth today believed. He went on to proclaim further that he was at this trial to show up fundamentalism and to prevent bigots and ignoramuses from controlling the educational systems in the country. And Bryan, shaking his fists at Darrow, cried out that he was there to protect the Word of God against the greatest atheist and agnostic in the United States — Darrow!

68

It was a savage duel between the two men with Bryan coming out on the short end of the acrimonious encounter. The fact was that the fundamentalist faith which Bryan represented could not take the witness stand and face up to the reason and skill of a person like Darrow.

Two million words were telegraphed out of Dayton, and radio station WGN of Chicago broadcast into American homes one of the strangest trials which had ever taken place in a court of law.

Despite the pros and cons, the fact still remained that Scopes did teach about evolution in the classroom and that was against the law of the State of Tennessee. He was found guilty and fined $100.

Within a week after the trial was over, Dayton began to return to its normal sleepy self as the cast of characters disappeared into history. Bryan died eight days after the trial at the age of sixty-five. He felt that even though his religion was old fashioned and out of date, he would nevertheless, be its champion or would die trying.

Darrow died of old age in 1938. And Scopes? He gave up teaching and went to work as a geologist for an oil company. In 1955, interest in the trial came back because of a stage play called "Inherit the Wind." In 1967, Scopes, who was then retired, wrote his reminiscences of the trial in a book called *Center of the Storm*. Although Scopes never uttered one word at his trial, in his book he stated that he felt the main issue was not religion but was the principle of the separation of Church and State. He wrote: "If the state was allowed to dictate what a teacher must teach (a subject in accordance with the beliefs of one particular religion) then the state could force schools to teach the belief of the person in power, which could lead to oppression of all personal religious liberties." Scopes died at the age of seventy on October 21st, 1970 at Shreveport, Louisiana.

And what happened to everyone else who had come to Dayton for the trial; the reporters, the moviemen, the syndicated writers and the telegraph operators? They shook the dust of Dayton, Tennessee out of their clothes and mind. The "Monkey Trial" as it became known, had been a good show for the front pages, but it was time to file the story away in the history books and move on to something else. As for the fight between the fundamentalist and the modernist approach to the Bible, it still goes on.

As the Scopes trial became a memory, another trial jumped into the public spotlight. It was the trial of Colonel Billy Mitchell by the United States Army on the charges of insubordination and conduct prejudicial to the service.

Mitchell went into the army when the Spanish-American War broke out in 1898. He was an eighteen year old lad at the time and had been a junior at Columbia University. He entered the army as a private but after seven days made second lieutenant. After the war with Spain, he served in the Philippines under General Arthur MacArthur. In 1909, he graduated from the Army Staff College at Fort Leavenworth, Kansas and in 1915, he was assigned to the aviation section of the Army Signal Corps.

Prior to the United States entering World War I, he was sent to France as an observer. When the United States became involved in the conflict, Mitchell became the first United States airman to fly over enemy lines, and he also was one of the most decorated men in the American Expeditionary Forces. He was promoted to Brigadier General and after the war he returned to the United States to take up a post as Assistant Chief of United States Air Services. In this capacity he devoted himself to the promotion of aviation, became a vociferous speaker and wrote books on the subject of the future of the aeroplane.

He was an outspoken critic of the United States Navy, and said that they could not defend America's coast from an attack by aircraft. As Mitchell put it, "the Navy's battleships were obsolete," and if the Navy had any judgment at all it would construct a ship which would be capable of launching and landing aircraft. He called it an aircraft carrier.

His struggle for airpower took on the characteristics of a challenge to sea power. To prove his point that aircraft could sink a battleship, a test was set up near Hampton Roads, Virginia. There an old captured German battleship, the *Ostfriesland*, built in World War I and designed by the Germans to be unsinkable, would be the target ship to see if Mitchell could prove his case. Mitchell did. On the third and final attack, the battleship *Ostfriesland* turned over and sank. Mitchell had set out to prove the supremacy of airpower and he had succeeded. Needless to say the Navy came up with its own version of the sinking of the battleship. They pointed out that if the ship had been moving instead of being anchored, and had the ship been firing back at the attacking planes, the results would not have been the same. Therefore, the Navy concluded, the test proved nothing. Nevertheless, Mitchell persisted in irritating everybody. He told everyone who would listen to him that the United States, in order to protect its shores, must have an air force capable of flying out and destroying an enemy before it could get close to our coast. To silence Mitchell, the government sent him on a tour of the Pacific and Orient. He was to inspect the United States Air Services and to investigate air activities of Japan and China.

Mitchell was so impressed with the Japanese build-up of air-power that when he returned from his tour of the Pacific, he predicted that Japan would one day with its airpower, attack the United States possession at Pearl Harbor, Hawaii. Therefore, he went on to say, to protect the country we should build ships capable of landing and launching aircraft and have an adequate airforce to defend our shores from any attack.

There was no doubt about the fact that Mitchell was now getting on the nerves of his superiors as he was demoted to the rank of colonel and assigned to duty at a remote outpost of civilization at a place called Fort Sam Houston, in Texas.

But this did not silence Mitchell. When a great air disaster took place and one of his best friends went down with the dirigible *Shenandoah*, which was torn apart by a storm as it made its way across the midwest to put on a display for a state fair, Mitchell issued a public statement which would initiate his court martial. He stated: "This accident is the direct result of the incompetence, the criminal negligence, and the almost treasonable negligence of our national defense by the Navy and War Departments in their attempt to keep down the development of aviation. I can stand by no longer and see these disgusting performances take place at the expense of the lives of our people and to the disillusionment of the American public."

William "Billy" Mitchell, who prophetically warned that a strong air defense was critical to the nation's survival.

Mitchell had deliberately put himself in a position for either a court martial or reprimand. He hoped to have a trial so he could prove his ac-

71

cusations against the Navy and War Departments. He further hoped to stir public opinion to do something about the decaying policies toward airpower in the country. Mitchell got his wish as President Coolidge ordered him back to Washington, D.C. and set October 28th, 1925 for his court martial.

Mitchell got two of his friends, Frank Reid and Clayton Bissell (both experts on aviation), to defend him. Reid and Bissell agreed that Mitchell was guilty of violating the 96th Article of War as charged, but they also agreed that the trial should be used to educate the American public on the necessity of aviation for our national defense.

At the old Armory Building in Washington, D.C. the trial got underway. The defense opened with a plea for dismissal of the case. They stated that Mitchell was merely exercising the right of freedom of speech and if the First Amendment didn't apply to the Army why didn't the Constitution say so? But the court martial board would not accept the idea of having the charges dismissed and continued the trial as the prosecutor read the 96th Article of War. It was an all-encompassing law that gave the Army almost unlimited authority. According to this article, all the prosecution had to do was to show that Mitchell by his statement had discredited the service and was guilty of the charges of insubordination and conduct prejudicial to the service.

At the trial which lasted until December 17th, 1925, the defense attorneys tried to prove that everything Mitchell had stated would come true, while all the prosecution had to prove was that he had been insubordinate.

Mitchell was found guilty of violating the 96th Article of War and was sentenced to immediate suspension from rank and command with forfeiture of all pay and allowances. President Coolidge upheld the court martial decision, and the only thing left for Mitchell to do was to resign from the service which he did in February of 1926.

After he resigned from the service, as a private citizen he tirelessly continued to campaign for the airpower that he felt the United States must have in case it became involved in another war.

Then came the crash of the stock market in 1929, which was followed by the great depression. The public's attention shifted to other and more pressing problems than national defense and during the 1930s, Mitchell died of complications from influenza.

And so it would be that Billy Mitchell brought disgrace on himself to prove to his countrymen that they would need to have an unsurpassed airforce to defend themselves in the future from any would-be invader.

Just so you won't think that this one man's crusade was in vain, in July of 1926, the Congress created something called the Army Air Corps and by 1932, the United States Navy launched its first aircraft carrier . . . the *USS Ranger*. And, oh yes! All the other predictions Mitchell made did come to pass. The Japanese *did* attack and *did* sink the United States battleship fleet at Pearl Harbor, Hawaii and yes, it was airpower which did win the war for civilization and mankind as Mitchell predicted it would.

In rememberance for what Billy Mitchell did, in 1946, the Congress of the United States authorized the mint to strike a medal in his honor. It was a medal which commemorated the struggle for the things in which he believed, gave recognition for his foresight and pioneering service to aviation, and honored him for his devotion to the people of this country for whom he was willing to wreck his career and give his life.

On the commercial side of things, by October of 1925, the great-get-rich-quick Florida land boom was at its peak. Hard-headed men and women were exposed to the most delirious fever of real estate speculation that had ever attacked the United States. The Florida land boom speculation is said to have exceeded any gold rush or any other business stampede in the history of the country to that time.

The Dixie highway was clogged with automobiles from every part of the country as people wanted to get near Miami. Why? Because the whole strip of the Florida coast line from Palm Beach southward was going to be developed into an American Riviera. What you had to do was to get there first and get in on the ground floor. You would purchase your land as cheaply as you could, sit on it for a month or so and then sell it to somebody else for double what you paid for the land originally. Boy! What a way to make some quick easy money!

What caused the Florida land boom? First there was Florida's great climate and its accessibility for people living in the cold northeastern part of the United States who wanted to live in this warm-weather-paradise. Second, there was the fact that the automobile was rapidly making nomads out of Americans. Third, there was great confidence in the Coolidge prosperity by the people and fourth was advertising. So, the public bought. They would buy anything anywhere so long as it was in Florida. All one had to do was to announce a new development, be it honest or be it fraudulent, and if it was in Florida, people scrambled to buy up lots. It was no wonder that Miami became known as the "Fair White Goddess of Cities."

But as usual, sooner or later booms turn to busts and in the case of the Florida land boom, it was sooner. In 1926, two major hurricanes showed what a soothing tropical breeze could do when it got a running start from the West Indies. The hurricanes were the worst Florida had ever witnessed. Damage was so severe that the Red Cross ran out of funds to help the homeless. The hurricanes caused the death of 372 persons, destroyed over 5,000 homes, left 18,000 families homeless and caused property damage which was estimated to be in excess of $80,000,000.

By 1927, as one approached Miami by road, he saw dead subdivisions and half obliterated names on crumbling gates. The development of Florida as a paradise in which to live would have to wait for the future.

Despite the failure of the Florida land boom, prosperity for the most part existed throughout the rest of the country. There were plenty of jobs and most of the working people had plenty of money to spend. In 1923, United States Steel abandoned the twelve-hour day seven-day week and then, much to the shock of the industrial community, Henry Ford instituted his eight-hour day five-day week for the people who worked for him. Labor leaders were quick to congratulate Ford for his avant-garde thinking, as they felt the new work week would be a means to check overproduction and limit unemployment. Then International Harvester Company, not to be outdone by Ford, announced something even more electrifying. They were going to give their employees a two week annual vacation with pay! Incredible.

Construction during the 1920s also seemed to have no end to it, as during that decade New York City got a brand new skyline. If Europeans who had traveled to the United States in 1910 were awed by twenty-story skyscrapers with elevators in them, when they returned to the United States in the late twenties they would have been struck dumb to find that the old buildings were dwarfed by new giants. High above the city streets, helmeted workers balanced themselves on girders as taller and taller the buildings soared. The skyscraper became a radiant defiant display of American energy and optimism to the world. It was an expression of the ebullient spirit as was the gothic cathedral to the Medieval Age of Europe.

Into this wonder world came Sister Aimee Semple McPherson. Aimee was born in Canada in 1890. She grew up on hard work and religion, and in 1907 at the age of seventeen she married an itinerant Pentecostal minister by the name of Robert Semple. Aimee followed her husband wherever he went to do his work, and while he was preaching in China tragedy struck. Her husband was stricken with what was called eastern fever and died one month after Aimee gave birth to her first child. Upon her return to the United States, Aimee sought to recapture the elusive bluebird of happiness and since loneliness was obviously unendurable to her, she married once again. This time she married a grocery clerk by the name of Harold Mc Pherson. She had a child by this union but unfortunately, the marriage eventually ended in an unhappy divorce.

Then Aimee got the call to preach the Word of God and by becoming a traveling evangelist, she set forth on a venture of soul saving. Lugging her children along and with the usual paraphernalia of a traveling evangelist, a car and a tent, she preached in the north in the summer and in the south in the winter. Each year her technique became better, and it was during this time in her life that she formulated her Foursquare Gospel Creed; which was infallibility of the Bible, conversion, physical healing by religious means and the personal return of Jesus Christ to this earth.

She published a little magazine, the *Foursquare Monthly* and began to acquire a small but loyal following. Soon the crowds got bigger and bigger and the tent gave way to lecture halls. Then, the lecture halls gave way to city auditoriums.

In San Diego, California at Balboa Park in 1921, Aimee was lifted out of the run of the mill small-timers into the big time. 30,000 people attended this meeting and it was here that her first sensational "miracle" took place. A middle-aged paralytic rose from her wheelchair and took a few stumbling steps. When the audience saw this they all came forth to be baptized by Sister Aimee. Never once did Sister Aimee contend that she was a miracle worker or that she could actually heal the sick. As she put it, "I am not the healer. Jesus is the healer. I am only the person who opens the door and says come in."

From that time on Sister Aimee was famous. And since she was doing so well, why not build a temple? So it was that Sister Aimee built her temple and held revival meetings on a year round basis. On January 1st, 1923, the Angelus Temple was opened near the rushes of Echo Park Lake in Los Angeles, California. There, trumpeters blared out majestic sounds and Aimee pulled the string that unveiled an electrically illuminated rotating cross, atop the temple, that could be seen at night for a distance of fifty miles. The temple cost $1,500,000, had a seating capacity of 5,000 persons, a $75,000 broadcasting station, a great commissary, a theological seminary with hundreds of students, a vast organ, and a collection of costumes for Aimee and her choir. From the time the temple was open, a group of templites in relay teams prayed continuously, day and night in response to tens of thousands of requests for prayers.

At the temple, Aimee proceeded to entertain people who came to see

75

her with pageants, picture slides of the Holy Land, musically dramatized sermons, and of course healing sessions. Before her death in 1944, she baptized over 40,000 people in the temple. She established four hundred branch churches or as she called them "lighthouses" and located one hundred seventy eight missionary stations throughout the world.

Aimee's basic formula was . . . make things simple and easy to remember. To this she preached her four-square gospel. But the most important factor in her success was the way in which she substituted cheerfulness for gloom. She gave people love and happiness, relaxed them and released their minds from the frightful visions of eternal damnation. In the place of these frightful visions, she gave the people flowers, music, golden trumpets, choirs, and angels. Furthermore, Aimee was in the right place to be an angel of joy as during the decade from 1920-1930, hordes of new residents moved into Los Angeles. Most of the people who moved to Los Angeles during this period of time were from small towns and farming areas in the mid-west. They were aching with loneliness and wanted to know someone. They found their heart's desire at the Angelus Temple in Sister Aimee where they shared happiness . . . the happiness of kindred souls.

Aimee was just what they needed and at the close of each of her sermons, she would ask the sinners to come forward and be saved. It was done in a flare of fashion and pageantry. On one occasion, Aimee staged a fourteen hour Holy Ghost rally of continuous preaching with a team of preachers spelling each other. If a minister collapsed with fatigue, Aimee would leap up and take his place.

There was no doubt about the fact that Aimee entertained the folks, but she had a message they wanted to hear. The post war period was full of restlessness and there was a craze for entertainment and a passion for frivolity. All of this gave birth to something called the "Jazz Age." The flapper had arrived . . . a little tipsy, with short skirts and bobbed hair. It was a time for petting and necking, for hip flasks and roadside taverns, for movie palaces, and Hollywood movies filled with scandals and commotion. All America seemed to be stepping out on an emotional binge and Sister Aimee Semple McPherson was determined to lead those people who wanted to be saved to heaven.

So it was that Sister Aimee, who arrived in Los Angeles in 1921, with one hundred dollars and a broken down car, by 1926 owned a temple and a residence valued at over three million dollars. Aimee became more than just a household word in Los Angeles, she was a folk hero, a civic institution, and a patron saint. She breathed new life and meaning into an ancient and powerful story. The story was that of the miracle-worker, the faith healer, the one who comes to lift the people out of their bondage.

Then on May 18th, 1926, Sister Aimee disappeared. The newspapers had been carrying stories about Amundsen giving up his polar expedition, the American Embassy in Buenos Aires being bombed and President Coolidge returning to Washington, D.C. after a cruise on the Presidential yacht the *Mayflower*. On the back pages of the papers were stories of stunts, escapades, and broken records. There were stories of prosperity ablaze on the land and rum-runners with flashlights and machine guns busy getting their merchandise ashore at Malibu. But now all the headlines screamed that Sister Aimee had gone swimming at Venice Beach near Los Angeles and had vanished! Late afternoon extras told that Sister Aimee was gone.

Thousands of people gathered about the temple and near the beach where Aimee had disappeared. For thirty-two days the armies of the faithful kept a night and day prayer vigil going at the temple. Bonfires were built on the beach, people wept, prayed, moaned, and sang hymns. Patrols were sent up and down the beach, airplanes swept low over the water, and deep sea divers prowled the ocean floor. Then an ecstatic follower felt she glimpsed an image of Aimee on the bright shimmering waters of the Pacific and was forcefully restrained from plunging into the water. One young man by the name of Robert Browning, however, jumped into the sea crying out at the top of his lungs, "I'm going after her." He drowned before he could be dragged out of the surf.

Then all of a sudden the newspapers picked up the scent of scandal. Did Sister Aimee die in the surf or was she just trying to get away alone with Kenneth Ormiston who ran the radio station at the Angelus Temple?

With everybody now looking for her, Aimee decided that she should return. On the morning of June 23rd, Sister Aimee stumbled out of the darkness and knocked on the door of a cottage in Agua Prieta, Mexico which is across the border from Douglas, Airzona. Once discovered, Aimee told a lurid tale of being kidnapped and held in detention. She gave a fanciful account of the kidnappers who were Rose, Steve, and Jake. The story was in almost every newspaper throughout the country. Aimee's disappearance and return was one of the greatest stories of the twenties, for it contained all the right ingredients! It had sex, mystery, underworld characters, spooks, kidnappers, the ocean, the hot desert sand, escape, and a thrilling finale.

Over a period of time Aimee's story was exposed as a crazy hoax. The public, with its passion for scandal inflamed and its appetite for sensationalism whetted, was like a pack of salacious hounds baying about Aimee, eager for a kill. They wanted to force Aimee to confess her sins, to make public the intimacies of her love life and the spicy details of the time, the place, and the circumstances.

There was a trial in Los Angeles where the enemies of Aimee charged her as being a charlatan. But the trial was never concluded as all charges against her were dropped. Aimee took this as a vindication. As soon as the case against her was dismissed, she departed on a national "rehabilitation tour." But much to her surprise, the tour misfired. Somehow Sister McPherson was now just plain Aimee. The one time miracle worker had become a woman of notoriety. In cities where she had scored her greatest evangelical triumphs, she was now greeted with relative indifference as she spoke to half-empty halls. From that time on there was nothing but a mounting sense of insecurity, exhaustion, and despair for Aimee.

Evangelist Aimee Semple McPherson during one of her court appearances.

Then too, when the stock market crashed, demolishing the crazy structure of the Coolidge prosperity, new messiahs made their appearances in Southern California. Upton Sinclair promised to End Poverty in California. Dr. Francis Townsend of Long Beach promised pensions for the aged, and Willis and Lawrence Allen promoted their "Ham and Eggs or thirty dollars every Thursday" scheme. Yet, in those troubled times Aimee managed to survive and hold a remnant of her following together, even though her flock was now reduced to between eight and ten thousand people. But she was somehow out of date . . . you know . . . old hat . . . a bit of a bore. She was no longer a world famous evangelist but just another whacky person.

Sister Aimee lasted through the thirties and in September of 1944, she passed away. Her funeral was one of the most heavily attended services ever held in California. The eulogy was delivered by Howard P. Courtney of Los Angeles who described Aimee as a young country girl who was now entering God's Hall of Fame. And so it was that Aimee Semple McPherson, a woman who believed with all her heart in goodness and kindness; who aroused so much love and devotion in the hearts of thousands of little people; and who for a moment in her own life sought to find some happiness for herself by stepping out of character, did enter God's Hall of Fame. But for those who remember the twenties, they can still see in their minds, Sister Aimee chasing the devil with a pitchfork and allowing sunlight to come into the souls of those she had touched.

One of the major contributions to the prosperity of the "Roaring Twenties" was the construction of roads and highways which poured fresh public funds into the economy. Highway construction programs employed more men and spent more money than any single private industry. In 1914 there were very few good roads outside the east coast; crossing the continent was a real adventure, as during the spring when the snow melted or after a good rain storm, automobiles would sink into gumbo mud up to their hubs. Travelers crossing Iowa or Nebraska were often forced to wait several days until the roads dried before moving on to the next town. Roads were in such poor condition because automobiles were viewed as pleasure vehicles and state legislatures were reluctant to vote public funds to improve roads for just a few. But in 1924, the Federal Road Act offered federal money to states which would organize highway departments and match federal funds. Spurred on by this federal money, every section of the country launched ambitious road building programs during the twenties. By 1928, tourists could drive from New York City to St. Mary, Kansas on paved roads. Yes! Paved roads.

Much of the roar of the twenties came from the internal combustion engine as without the new automobile industry, the prosperity of the decade would scarcely have been possible, as the development of the auto industry in a single generation was probably the greatest single achievement of modern technology. In 1900 there was not a single filling station in the country at all, but by 1902, some were found in San Francisco and other major cities, and the speed limit in most of these places was held to a rip roaring eight miles per hour. Furthermore, in 1900 there were only about 4,000 cars in the country, as compared to 4,800,000 by the end of the 1920s. The fact was there was almost one car per family in the United States as the decade of the twenties closed. There was scarcely a corner of the American economy which the automobile industry did not touch. It stimulated the oil industry to find more liquid gold, it boosted road construction, extended the housing boom into the suburbs and developed new businesses.

Detroit became the Mecca of the modern world and Henry Ford became the greatest prophet of the industry. On the one hand Ford was the builder and bulwark of the modern, mechanized United States. On the other hand, he devoted his efforts and money to sustaining old-fashion America with its tried and true morals and manners. He grew up on a farm, had an eighth grade education, moved to Detroit, Michigan, became an apprentice mechanic, and by 1896 put together his first automobile. Shortly thereafter, Ford had his car doing ninety miles per hour and from this, his rise to an industrial giant took place. But although Henry Ford left the farm, the farm never left Henry. The agrarian ideas and values he had learned on the farm shaped his thoughts and actions even after he became the Industrial King of the United States. Soon industrial missions came from all over the mechanized world to study his techniques. Ford, the man who personified the farm-boy mechanic, in a single lifetime had reached the top. His was the Horatio Alger story of rags to riches. He fulfilled the American dream of an acquisitive society committed to the belief of individual advancement and the rugged self-made man. Ford not only brought the automobile to the masses of the world, but he was viewed as the magical tinkerer who revolutionized human life. He was the high priest of mass production, which people of the world saw to be more important than any ideological doctrine as the solution to the curse of world poverty. Henry Ford was worshipped as the industrial miracle-maker and was voted by college students during the twenties as one of the greatest figures of all time, surpassed only by Christ and Napoleon.

It is no wonder that Henry Ford's hour of destiny had come and that he rode in the position of honor. In 1913 it required twelve hours to make a car but the year after he introduced his assembly line techniques, Ford was able to drop that time to about ninety minutes. Finally by 1920, Ford achieved his life long dream by building one car for every minute of the working day. Now you can see why Henry Ford, by the end of the twenties, was a legend, a folk hero, and the symbol of the new international industrialism. Not only did he put the nation on wheels but he changed the face of the country as well. By the end of the 1920s, paved roads, repair shops, and filling stations had become so plentiful that any motorist might sally forth on a day's journey without fear of being stuck in a mudhole, stranded without benefit of gasoline or crippled by a dead spark plug. Automobiles were now made with such precision that many motorists hardly knew what a spark plug looked like, and with the advent of the self-starter (invented by Charles Kettering), women could now wheel a car down the roads. Driving was no longer just a man's world after Kettering's invention, and now that cars were closed to the outside weather, motorists had no need for spartan or pioneer blood to drive in the cold weather of January.

With the invention of pyroxylin finishes, cars broke out in a whole rainbow of colors. Before, the customer had just one choice . . . black! Not only that, but cars were now being designed lower to the ground as designers sought new harmonies of line and balloon tires were introduced to give a smoother ride. By 1926, the Flivver (the Model T Ford) was no longer selling. People were no longer content with Ford's Model T and its maximum speed of forty-five miles per hour. They were no longer content to move slowly uphill in the Flivver with their weary left foot jammed against the low speed pedal while some robin's-egg blue Chevrolet roared past them in second gear. So Henry Ford capitulated to the new times and decided to produce a brand new car.

Everyone wondered what miracle Ford would come up with as he shut down his huge plant, scrapped his Model T and brought in new machines to produce a new and better car. The country was in a state of suspense. When the new car was taken out on a trial run and a photographer got a picture of it, it was published in every newspaper, and readers avidly discussed every line of this new beauty.

Then, in huge newspaper ads, the Ford Motor Company announced that the new Ford (the Model A as it was called) would be ready for the public market on December 2nd, 1927. Over 500,000 people across the United States made a down payment on the car without seeing it, without knowing what it could do or even what the price tag would be.

When December 2nd, 1927 did come, over 100,000 people in Detroit flocked into company showrooms and mounted police had to be called out to patrol the crowds. In Kansas City, the mobs were so great that at the convention hall where the car was being shown, platforms had to be built to lift the new car high enough off the ground so everyone could see it. It

Described as a "completely new car from radiator cap to rear axle," the Model A was powered by a 40 horsepower engine and was capable of speeds of 55-60 miles per hour.

went like that from one end of the country to the other. Thousands of orders came in for Niagara Blue roadsters and Arabian Sand Phaetons. The unveiling of the new Ford was one of the great events of 1927.

With these new automobiles, the face of America changed drastically. Villages on route 66 bloomed. Garages, filling stations, hot dog stands, bill board signs, chicken dinner restaurants, tea rooms, tourist's rest stops, and camp sites sprang up everywhere. In San Luis Obispo, California, the first motel opened. It was called Heinemann's Motel and all a person had to do was to drive his car to a cottage like building, park, go inside, and get a good night's sleep. The interurban trolley perished. Railroads gave up branch lines and saw their revenues slowly dwindle to the competition of cars, busses, and trucks which snorted along the concrete highways. By the end of the twenties, a single traffic officer was not enough to handle the traffic and everywhere one saw the advent of red, yellow, and green stop and go lights, one way streets, boulevard stops and not enough parking places. The age of the gasoline engine had arrived.

After having established the automobile as a way of life for Americans, Henry Ford next turned his talents toward farming. He told a group of people that he himself had traveled ten thousand miles behind a plow and hated every minute of the grueling grind of farm work. He now addressed himself to the problem of industrializing agriculture. His tractors replaced the horses. Mechanization made it possible to produce in twenty days working time what formerly had required a year. For all of this Ford won another title . . . "The Father of Modern Agriculture." Henry Ford testified to the nations ability to move into the future without losing the values of the past.

During the 1920's, the Fordson tractor won almost every plowing and endurance contest it entered. Here, Henry Ford and his son Edsel pose in front of one of their tractors at a midwestern fair.

During the 1920s, in cities and towns throughout the country, electricity made its debut in more and more American homes. This meant that not only could lights be used, but so could a wide range of electrical appliances. Women could buy vacuum cleaners, washing machines, toasters, and electric sewing machines. Being in debt was no longer regarded as being shameful as people bought anything their heart's desired on the installment plan. The fact of the matter was, Americans were purchasing things with their paychecks that they never before had been able to buy.

As for entertainment and amusement, most Americans on the weekends would go to the ball park or would walk down to the neighborhood theater to see the latest movie. There, one could see the faces of Charlie Chaplin, Harold Lloyd, the Keystone Cops, Gloria Swanson, Douglas Fairbanks, or Rudolph Valentino carrying a blond heroine across a burning desert to fling her into his tent. Most of the gals in the theater would swoon while the men, naturally, would scoff.

By 1927, the Academy of Motion Picture Arts and Sciences was established. It was comprised of all levels of studio personnel from actors to set designers to give honors and recognition to noteworthy achievements in the motion picture industry. The award given by the academy was called an Oscar and the first Oscar given was for a motion picture called *Wings* which was a story of the aerial war of planes in World War I.

Then Warner Brothers Motion Picture Studio produced the first talking motion picture. The sound track was actually on the film and the actor's lips moved in synchronization with the sound. Before this, movies were silent, and most theaters had a musician who played the piano or organ. It was his job to create the mood for the audience as depicted on the screen. In 1926, sound was introduced to movies by having the projectionist play a record. It was hoped by all that he would be able to get the movement of the lips to coincide with the words which the actors uttered. The first movie to use sound by use of the phonograph was shown in the Warner Theater in New York City and the motion picture was *Don Juan*, starring John Barrymore. As you can guess, this system did not work well at all because the sound track seldom followed the movement of the actor's lips and it drove the audiences crazy. But now in 1927, in the motion picture *The Jazz Singer* starring Al Jolson, everything was synchronized. Jolson sang a song and the sound coming out of the speaker behind the screen matched the movement of his mouth perfectly. Talking movies were here! With the coming of sound to motion pictures, many actors and actresses could not make the transition from silent to talking movies as their voices were either too high or too displeasing to the audiences and some of filmdom's biggest names faded from sight.

Despite the fact that movies were becoming more and more popular, vaudeville was still the greatest audience attraction with big name stars like Jack Benny, George Burns and Gracie Allen, the Marx Brothers, Gallagher and Shean, Bob Hope, and Will Rogers headlining the theater marquees. Vaudevillians played in theaters from town to town always hoping to make it to the big time. You knew you had arrived when you received a telegram from New York City asking you to appear in the Ziegfeld Follies, as Flo Ziegfeld produced the most outstanding extravaganzas ever seen, and only with the top talent. But when the Great Depression came the follies did not survive and in 1931, they opened for the last time. They were not a success and Ziegfeld died broke and bankrupt. Then in the spring of 1932, vaudeville went to its grave when the Palace Theater in New York City gave its last all vaudeville bill.

Besides the movies, radio also provided entertainment for the American people. If you couldn't afford to go to a movie, you could sit at home and listen to the radio programs which seemed to be getting better and better. Why, you could hear Roxy and his gang, the Cliquot Club Eskimos, or the A & P Gypsies. If you liked sports, you could listen to Grantland Rice broadcast a baseball game. Then, there was Floyd Gibbons who narrated the news and of course you might listen to the greatest radio singer and the most idolized warbler of the 1920s — Rudy Vallee. But for sheer comedy, the comedians Freeman Gosden and Charles Correll produced one of the most listened-to programs on the air . . . Amos'n Andy. The program took the country by storm. People wouldn't answer their phones during the program and movie theaters would interrupt their shows and tune in the broadcast for their audiences. All of this radio entertainment was free, given to you by sponsors who wanted to advertise their products with the hope that you would purchase their goods the next time you went shopping.

The salesmen of the 1920s used a wide variety of methods to sell their products. One of the things a radio listener would hear would be an ominous voice warning "Four out of Five Have It!" Have what? According to the advertising men four out of five people had pyorrhea. It was an inflammation of the sockets of the teeth. In magazine ads you would see some poor fellow (one of the four who had it) covering his lower face with a white mask which would mercifully conceal his unhappy mouth. The caption would read . . . "He used to be a leader, but now he is a follower." By using Forhan's toothpaste you could prevent tooth neglect which caused pyorrhea.

Then there was the ad to sell Life-Buoy soap. The ad read "Even your best friend won't tell you." Won't tell you what? Won't tell you that you have B.O. (body odor). If you were listening to this ad on the radio, when the person said "B.O." a fog horn would sound The ad went on to tell you that if you did have "B.O." you offended people around you. The only way to stop being offensive was to bathe with Life-Buoy soap as it would wash away the bacteria which caused "B.O."

Another gem asked, "When you are talking to somebody, do they wilt and turn away?" If they do, you have halitosis (bad breath) which is caused by germs in your mouth. It was halitosis that led Gerhart Lambert to establish a company which made a product designed to eliminate these germs. The product? Listerine Antiseptic of course. According to the ads, all you would have to do is to gargle with Listerine and the germs which caused the bad

85

breath would be gone. No more would people say about a young lady that she was "Often a bridesmaid but never a bride." And why was this the case? The reader was led to believe it was because she had bad breath which drove the boys away from her. Or in the man's case, the ad would read "Why did she leave him?" Again the conclusion the reader was to draw was obvious. The person had bad breath and only Listerine Antiseptic could restore sunshine to his personal life.

If all this wasn't bad enough, the people of the twenties were also made aware of their manners by advertising men as ads promoting etiquette books read, "When the guests are gone, are you sorry you ever invited them? Be free from embarrassment. Let our famous book of etiquette tell you exactly what to do, say, write, or wear on every occasion." Yep, there wasn't nothin' better than good fetchin' up!

Americans during the twenties, more than ever before, became sports conscious and it is therefore understandable why historians have sometimes referred to the 1920s as the "Golden Age of Sports."

Why all of a sudden was there this interest in sports? Why did the American people become so sports-minded? Many feel that the American people were tired of the problems of the world which followed the Great War and turned to sports as an outlet for their emotions. Not only that, but they also had more money and more leisure time to spend watching sports. To make sure everybody knew what was happening, sports writers dramatized the spectacular feats of all sports.

In baseball, one man seemed to dominate the scene. He was George Herman Ruth, better known as the "Babe." He held the record for the most home runs ever hit in a career with a total of 714, and his record stood until 1974 when Henry (Hank) Aaron of the Atlanta Braves finally passed the Babe's mark. During his day, Ruth also held the records for the most home runs ever hit in one season (60), for extra base hits and for the most strike outs. Besides Ruth, there were other heroes of baseball like Ty Cobb, Tris Speaker, Walter Johnson, Grover Cleveland Alexander, George Sisler, Rogers Hornsby, Lou Gehrig, and Jimmy Foxx. With stars like these on every team, the fans jammed the grandstands to enjoy our national pastime.

Football was also on the rise and the man who was the greatest figure of the sport was Knute Rockne, the coach of Notre Dame. From 1918 until his death in 1931, his teams won 105 games, lost 12 and tied 5. Rock's team of 1924 was the one most widely heralded as it possessed the fastest, smoothest working backfield in Notre Dame's history. They were so good that their opponents referred to them as the "Four Horsemen." In dramatic

"Babe" Ruth, apparently watching one more ball go out of the park!

lore the Four Horsemen of the Apocalypse were Death, Destruction, Pestilence, and Famine. But during the 1920s they were Jim Crowley and Don Miller (halfbacks), Elmer Layden (fullback) and Harry Stuhldreher (quarterback). These backs played behind a line which was called the Seven Mules and when you put the entire team together, you had what sports writers called "The South Bend Cyclone."

And then there was Roy Riegles playing for the University of California on January 1st, 1929 in the Rose Bowl against Georgia Tech, who ran 70 yards the wrong way and won the game for his opponents. It was in the second quarter that California was on the offensive and lined up in a single wing. The center snapped the ball to Charlie Erb who was to hand it off to Riegles, but after the ball was snapped from center, it was bobbled in the backfield before Riegles got it. Despite all of this fumbling in the backfield, Riegles got the hand-off of the unstable football and headed down field in the right direction. He ran for four or five yards before he saw two Georgia Tech players charging down on him from the right. He made a horseshoe pivot to avoid being tackled and as he made the pivot, he lost his bearings

87

and started running full speed the wrong way.

Benny Lom, the Bears left halfback, was the first one on the field to realize what was happening. He reacted immediately and took out after Riegles who had a sizeable head start. Lom should have been able to catch Riegles in 30 or 40 yards as he was the fastest player on the Bears team, but Riegles was grasping at the stuff of which heroes are made. Feeling that Lom was trying to block out any Georgia Tech man who might be catching up with him, Riegles ran all the harder. As Lom began to overtake Riegles, he began shouting, "You're going the wrong way! You're going the wrong way!" But because of the noise of the crowd, Riegles heard nothing. As Riegles neared the goal line, Lom finally overtook him and much to Riegles' surprise, tackled him. As he was going down Georgia Tech's Frank Waddly hit Riegles hard and pushed him into the end zone. Cal lost the game and Riegles never did live down the fact that he had run 70 yards the wrong way for a safety.

There were other greats in football who also captured the imagination of the fans, but none was more popular than the "Gallopping Ghost," Red Grange of Illinois. He was the most spectacular broken-field runner of his day and he made All-American for three years in a row (1923-1925). He went on into professional football with the Chicago Bears and did for pro-football what Ruth did for baseball.

In boxing during the 1920s, one name was "Mister Big." It was William Harrison Dempsey. He was better known as Jack Dempsey and was sometimes called the "Manassa Mauler." Dempsey brought a stampede to the box office and sports writers labeled him the most spectacular fighter of his time, for he was one of the hardest hitting fighters the ring had seen. In his fight with Louis Firpo, "The Wild Bull of the Pampas," the fans saw a typical Dempsey fight. Firpo was knocked down seven times in the first round and in turn he knocked Dempsey through the ropes and out of the ring. In the second round, Dempsey was brought to his knees but was able to get to his feet and finally flatten Firpo for keeps.

Dempsey was thought to be invincible, but in 1926, Gene Tunney proved otherwise by taking the title away from him. One year later on September 22, 1927, the rematch between the two men was scheduled. The fight was one of the most controversial ever fought and many boxing fans felt Dempsey should have been given the fight. It was the seventh round and that long count that most boxing fans remember. Graham MacNamee described that round as follows.

Jack Dempsey crouches to evade a left by Gene Tunney during the title match.

"Dempsey comes into Tunney with both hands. As they come out of the clinch, Tunney catches Dempsey on the face. Dempsey comes back with a hard right to Tunney's face . . . Gene felt that. Gene felt that ladies and gentlemen. Dempsey comes on through with a terrific right. He's got Tunney against the ropes. There's another right landing on the champion's jaw. A barrage of lefts and rights and *Tunney is down! Tunney is down! The referee had not yet begun to count* . . . He has not yet . . . Now, Now, five, six, seven . . . Dempsey's waiting for him. Eight . . . Tunney's up. Tunney's up on nine! The fight is continuing. Tunney's backing away. He's back peddling. He looks a little groggy. Dempsey's coming in trying to get to him. Tunney's back peddling."

When Dempsey knocked Tunney down, he neglected to go to a neutral corner of the ring as both fighters had agreed they would do before the fight. The referee would not begin his count while Tunney was down until Dempsey moved to a neutral corner. This gave Tunney four revitalizing seconds to come back from that knockdown. Tunney survived that round and went on to win the fight on points.

In golf, one name dominated the fairways and that name was Bobby Jones. Even though he never turned professional, from 1923 to 1930, he won thirteen national championships and in 1930, he won what was known as golf's grand slam. He won the British Amateur, the British Open, the United States Open, and the United States Amateur. Undoubtedly, Jones with his putter (which he called "Calamity Jane") was the best golfer, but the most colorful golfer of the twenties was Walter Hagen. Besides being a cut-up on the links, he won eleven major titles and came the closest to Jone's record.

On the tennis courts, the superstar was William Tilden. During the ten years of the 1920s, Tilden was National Singles Champion for seven years and for six years he played in the Davis Cup matches without a defeat. Sportswriters said he played the game like an artist.

As for the gals in tennis, the superstars were Helen Wills, Susanne Lenglen, and Molla Mallory. Of the three, it was Helen Wills who won most of the honors. She won the World Championship matches at Wimbleton four years straight, playing each final round without the loss of a single set.

Dynamic Johnny Weismuller became the greatest swimmer of his day by claiming sixty-seven swimming records during his prime. But the one who really caught the world's attention in swimming was a young lady by the name of Gertrude Ederle. Trudy as she was called (the daughter of a New York City delicatessen owner) became the first woman in history to swim the English Channel. On August 6, 1926, she swam the treacherous twenty-two mile channel between Cape Gris-Nez and Dover, triumphing over rip tides and choppy water, in the record time of fourteen hours and thirty-one minutes.

On the track, the "Flying Finn" Paavo Nurmi drew the crowds. Nurmi, who raced with a stopwatch in his hand, won four gold medals at the 1924 Olympics and left more records by defeating more men over more distances than any other runner in the history of track to that time.

Indeed! As in every era of time, sports will have its heroes, but the sports heroes of the twenties seem to be the ones whose memories live on forever.

If movies, radio or sports weren't enough to entertain you, there were other sideshows that would. During the twenties, people were astounded by a young man who made a great deal of money just by sitting atop a flagpole. Thousands of people stood and gaped at Alvin "Shipwreck" Kelley. Kelley was a former boxer and had fought under the name of "Sailor" Kelley. He had been knocked out so often that fans started shouting "the sailor's been shipwrecked again." Hence, he became known as "Shipwreck" Kelley.

He started his flagpole sitting career in Hollywood, California, hired by a theater to draw a crowd. The idea caught on and soon afterwards everyone started sitting on flagpoles, but it was Kelley who was booked by a score of hotels, theaters, and sideshows. There was money to be made in breaking records during the 1920s even if the achievement was only that of perching on a flagpole. In Baltimore, Maryland, Kelley sat atop a flagpole for twenty-three days and seven hours. He subsisted on liquids hoisted up to him in a bucket and hired a man to shout at him if he showed signs of dozing off to sleep for more than twenty minutes at one time. Since Kelley was balanced atop the flagpole on a small disk equipped with stirrups to keep him from falling off, he could not afford the advantage of deep sleep as he could slip off and tumble to his death.

Another craze which caught on during the twenties was the marathon dance. Of all the crazy competitions ever thought up, the marathon dance won by a considerable margin the award of lunacy. Yowsah! Yowsah! Yowsah!

The object of these strange contests was to see which couples could out dance, or perhaps it should be said out last all the other dancers on the floor. Across the country, men and women staggered to near-exhaustion to the tune of a fox trot played by some seedy little band. The dancers competed for the prizes which in some cases were as much as several thousand dollars and spectators came to see the antics of the performers. In order to keep their partners awake, dancers would kick and punch each other, sniff smelling salts and place ice packs on themselves. Some unprincipled contestants would slip their rivals drinks containing sleeping potions or laxatives. After seven or eight days of painful plodding, dancers would often start acting rather peculiarly. Girls would come to hate their partners so much that after a fifteen minute recess, which was allowed at different intervals, they would scream when they saw them. The longest dance on record was one which went on for 119 days in Chicago, Illinois in 1930.

In that era of the twenties when people loved an endurance contest of any sort, there was one which was the crowning achievement of the marathon craze. It was the 3,422 mile transcontinental foot race from Los Angeles, California to New York City. It started on March 4th, 1928 with 241 contestants, each of whom paid $100 to enter the race, and lasted until May 27th. It was a race which sports writers dubbed "The Bunion Derby."

C.C. Pyle who promoted the race expected to make a fortune by selling

Flagpole standing! Alvin "Shipwreck" Kelley the famous champion flag pole sitter did some flag pole standing as well!

programs to eager crowds, from the manufacturers of the shoes, the ointments and suntan oils being used by the participants and from cities through which the race was to be run. The Highway 66 Association pledged $66,000 to Pyle if he would steer the race their way as they felt it would bring fame and fortune to the towns along the route. Not only that, but Pyle also felt that he could glean money from spectators along the way by setting up sideshows.

It was a great idea, but it fell flat. On the first day the number of runners dwindled from 241 to 199. One contestant was bowled over by a hit-and-run motorist. Nevertheless, the poor devil got up and kept going. Pyle also had problems with the concessionaires who were supposed to feed the runners. When the concessionaires charged more than $2 per day for food (a prearranged fee), Pyle fired them and from that time on the participants ate what was called Mulligan Stew at practically every meal on unwashed plates. After all these setbacks town after town reneged on its agreement to pay Pyle for bringing the race their way, as the crowds they hoped to attract never materialized. The sad fact was, the Bunion Derby was a bust as runner after runner fell by the wayside with fallen arches and blistered feet.

After 84 days the last 55 runners limped into New York City's Madison Square Garden, where only about 4,000 people were waiting to see the surviving nuts who had started this race 573 hours, 4 minutes, and 34 seconds before. First place went to Andrew Payne of Claremore, Oklahoma who received $25,000 first prize money, "Long" John Salo of Passaic, New Jersey was second, winning $10,000, Philip Granville of Hamilton, Ontario, Canada was third, winning $5,000 and Mike Joyce of Cleveland, Ohio was fourth winning $2,500.

It would be safe to say that there was nothing epic about flagpole sitting, marathon dances, or the Bunion Derby. They were just freak shows to be watched in an idle moment by the people who lived during the 1920s.

If you were not inclined to listen to the radio, got to the movies or partake of any of the other crazes of the twenties, you could still read a good book as the 1920s produced great literature, and in 1926 the Book-of-the-Month-Club paved the way for a revolution in book selling and book publishing. By the end of its first year of existence, the Book-of-the-Month-Club had over 40,000 subscribers enrolled and this number increased yearly until today there are several million members in the club.

In 1921, while people were singing such favorites as "Look for the Silver Lining" and "Blue Moon," others were reading Eugene O'Neill's *Anna Christie*. It was a powerful drama of waterfront life, and catapulted O'Neill into international fame and a Pulitzer Prize.

In 1922, when the Lincoln Memorial was being dedicated in Washington, D.C., the best songs of the year were "April Showers" (sung by Al Jolson) and "Say It with Music." It was also this year that Sinclair Lewis wrote his book called *Babbitt* which was a satire of a small town, the life in it, and the psychological dramas that existed there at the time. If you had the time to go to a Broadway play, you would find that "Abbie's Irish Rose" by Anne Nichols opened in New York City. It played the longest run of any American stage play to that date and closed on October 22, 1927 after it had run a total of 2,327 performances. It was the story of love between a Jewish boy and an Irish girl, and brought out the theme of racial prejudice, especially in the characters of the two fathers.

1923 saw *Icebound* by Owen Davis win the Pulitzer Prize while "No, No Nanette" became the most popular musical comedy of the season with music by Vincent Youmans. The show's favorite song was "Tea for Two." Other popular songs of 1923 were "Yes, We Have No Bananas" and "Barney Google."

By 1924, Sigmund Romberg's "The Student Prince" was bringing in the crowds and Rudolf Friml produced "Rose Marie." The favorite songs which were on everybody's lips that year (besides "Rose Marie") were "Lady be Good," "Indian Love Call," "I'll See You in My Dreams," and "Yes Sir That's My Baby." It was also in 1924 that composer George Gershwin performed his "Rhapsody in Blue" for the first time. It became an immediate success. What Gershwin did in "Rhapsody in Blue" was to combine popular music with symphonic modes. On the stage, Maxwell Anderson's play "What Price Glory" was ranked near the top. The play was an unromantic treatment of the Great War which had just ended.

In 1925, Sinclair Lewis' *Arrowsmith* caught the public's imagination. Here Lewis turned from satire to a novel dealing with a quest for truth. The book was about an idealistic young man who had come from the Midwest to New York City and finally succumbed to the vices of big city life.

Also widely read was Theodore Dreiser's book *An American Tragedy*. It was the story of a weak youth who drifts into a dilemma from which he cannot extricate himself and commits the ultimate crime by murdering a girl who had shown him love.

F. Scott Fitzgerald also published his masterpiece *The Great Gatsby*. This work of Fitzgerald's has been looked upon as the epitome of the illusions of the "Roaring Twenties." The book's characters are found in the palatial mansions on Long Island where there are expensive parties, prohibition bootleggers, frustrated love affairs, and entangled marriages.

The top songs of 1925 were "Show Me the Way to Go Home" and "Collegiate."

In 1926, Admiral Byrd flew over the North Pole and Gertrude Ederle swam the English Channel. This was also the year when Ernest Hemingway published his novel *The Sun Also Rises* . . . the story of the "Lost Generation" cut off from all national and emotional ties as the hero wanders through France and Spain. Sidney Howard's book, *The Silver Cord* was also widely read. Here the reader wades through a most profound psychological drama of inverted mother-love, in which a mother loves her sons with such passion that in the end it destroys all their lives.

Then in 1927, when Colonel Lindbergh was the first person to receive the Distinguished Flying Cross for his solo flight across the Atlantic, people were held in wonderment as they read Thornton Wilder's book *The Bridge of San Luis Rey*. It was the story of five persons who were killed when the Bridge of San Luis Rey collapses while they are crossing it. The story traces the relationship of the five killed to a Divine Power that led them to the bridge at the moment it collapsed. On Broadway the musical "Show Boat" produced by Flo Ziegfeld, with music by Jerome Kern was packing in the people. Songs like "Old Man River," "Make Believe," and "Can't Help Lovin' That Man" made it a great hit.

But besides Lindbergh's flight and Henry Ford introducing his Model A, the biggest thing to rock the country in 1927 was the execution of Sacco and Vanzetti. For over seven years the guilt or innocence of these two men had been argued. Now they were dead.

The story of Sacco and Vanzetti goes back to the crisp morning of April 15th, 1920, when a brutal robbery took place at South Braintree, Massachusetts. Frederick A. Parmenter (paymaster for the Slater, Morril Shoe Company) and Allessandro Berandelli (a guard) were taking the company's payroll from the train station to the company's offices. As Parmenter and Berandelli walked up the hill from the station, they neared a man who was leaning against a fence. As they passed him, he pulled a pistol from under his coat and opened fire. Parmenter and Berandelli were killed and the murderers then took the payroll and drove off in a black touring car.

The brutality of the crime incensed the people of Massachusetts, who believed the crime was committed by a gang of Italians. Public sentiment, already running strong against aliens because of the Red Scare and the Palmer Raids, prompted the police to make an intensive search for the killers.

On May 5th, 1920, the police arrested two suspects, both of whom were known to be Italian anarchists. The two men arrested were Niccola Sacco and Bartholomeo Vanzetti, who at the time of their arrest were told that they were being detained as suspicious characters. They were not aware that they were being charged with the murders and robbery which had taken place at South Braintree until after being questioned by the police. The arrest of these two men, a good shoemaker, and a poor fish peddler was to culminate in the most controversial trial of the 1920s.

After the selection of the jury, the Commonwealth of Massachusetts opened its case at the city of Dedham on May 31st, 1921. The prosecution based its case on what looked like formidable evidence. The District Attorney had an eyewitness to the shooting and a gun found on Vanzetti at the time of his arrest. This supposedly connected the two men with the Italian gang which, it was felt, had committed the murder and robbery. There was a cap which was supposed to belong to Sacco and which was found at the scene of the crime, and the last bit of evidence was the fact that Vanzetti had just recently purchased a ticket to go back to Italy.

Sacco and Vanzetti, leaving court under armed guard. Vanzetti with the mustache is the second from the right. Sacco is the third from the right.

As the trail progressed, flaws in the prosecution's case began to appear. The first descriptions of Sacco and Vanzetti given by the witnesses did not even match them. Yet, despite this, a year after the crime had been committed, five different witnesses were able to give positive identification of the two men in court, even though they had seen the perpetrators of the crime for only a few moments. Yet, of the five witnesses, only one was able to put Sacco at the scene of the crime at the time it occurred.

Next the defense produced its own eyewitness who fully discredited the prosecution's eyewitnesses. A Mrs. Jenny Novelli, who was also a witness to the crime, stated positively that it was not Sacco or Vanzetti that she saw. Nicola Gratti, another witness to the crime and a person who had known Sacco many years earlier, swore under oath that Sacco was not one of the men he saw at the scene of the crime.

The defendants also had alibis and witnesses to back up their stories. Vanzetti states that he had been making his rounds with his fish cart at the time of the robbery and people who purchased fish from him that day backed that testimony. Sacco claimed he was having lunch with Mr. John Williams at the time of the crime and Mr. Williams corroborated his story.

The gun found on Vanzetti when he was arrested, which was the same make and caliber as the murder weapon, was never proven by ballistics to be the same gun which had killed the two men. The cap found at the scene of the crime, supposedly Sacco's, was much too small for his head when he tried it on in the court room.

Next the conduct of Webster Thayer, the trial judge, was also questionable. Evidence of his prejudice and unsuitability as a judge was shown at an earlier trial. On April 24th, 1920, the *Boston Herald* ran a story of how Judge Thayer had criticized a jury vehemently for acquitting a man who had been accused of criminal anarchy; Judge Thayer thought he should have been put away.

Sacco and Vanzetti were found guilty by the jury of the South Braintree robbery and murders and Judge Thayer pronounced a sentence of death on them. As the verdict was announced and the sentence was given, Sacco called out in a shaken voice . . . "You . . . You kill innocent men."

The case wasn't over yet, however. Appeal after appeal dragged on year after year and as it did the public's interest became aroused more and more. It was argued that two men like Sacco and Vanzetti had neither the stomach nor the know-how to carry out such a daring daylight robbery. Another thing that aroused the public sympathy for Sacco and Vanzetti, was the demeanor of the two men themselves. Vanzetti in particular was a clearly remarkable man, an intellectual of noble character, a philosophical anarchist of a type which it seemed impossible to associate with a payroll murder.

Seven long years went by as Judge Thayer stubbornly denied appeal after appeal. When the last appeal was denied, public opinion forced Governor Fuller of Massachusetts to review the case with the hope of a possible pardon for the men. The governor appointed an advisory committee to make a further study of the case. The committee consisted of men like President Lowell of Harvard University, President Stratton of the Massachusetts Institute of Technology and Judge Robert Grand all of whom were respected men of the community.

Unbelievably, a few weeks later, the committee reported that they believed Sacco and Vanzetti to be guilty. Instead of a pardon, Sacco and Vanzetti were now told that they would be executed on the night of August 22nd, 1927. The two men, who had gathered about their cause the hopes and fears of millions of people throughout the world, were to be sent to the electric chair.

With this announcement, the passions of the early 1920s were revived as pickets marched before the Boston State House calling on the Governor to release the two men. People once more found themselves in bitter argument over the identification of Sacco's cap and the value of Captain Proctor's testimony about the fatal bullet. Near rioting broke out when pickets outside the gates of the prison were arrested.

The fact of the matter was that these two hard working individuals had aroused more people to their cause than anyone could remember. And everyone also remembered the eloquence of Bartholomeo Vanzetti, who in his final statement said, "If it had not been for this thing, I might have lived out my life talking on street corners to scorning men. I might have died unmarked, unknown, a failure. Never in our full life could we hope to do such work for tolerance, for justice, and for man's understanding of men as now we do by accident. The taking of our lives . . . the lives of a good shoemaker and a fish peddler . . . ahh . . . that last moment belongs to us . . . that agony is our triumph."

Vanzetti's eloquence lasted but a fleeting moment as on the morning of August 23rd, 1927, headlines screamed throughout the country that he and Sacco were dead. A shiver and wonder went through everyone. Had justice been done or was this execution a hideous mistake?

As 1928 rolled around almost everyone's attention was focused on a new idea which would end all wars forever more. The idea was the Kellogg-Briand Peace Pact. At the Washington Naval Disarmament Conference of 1921-1922, the United States attempted to prevent future wars by limiting arms and signing pledges of nonaggression. With the Kellogg-Briand Peace Pact, America promoted the idea of a "Parchment Peace"; a peace built on paper promises that war would be abandoned entirely as an instrument of national policy. The idea of a treaty to outlaw war was the brain child of a civic-minded Chicago lawyer by the name of Solomon Levinson. The idea caught on and Professor J.T. Shotwell of Columbia University took up the standard and popularized it. He pointed out that during the previous decade there were laws of war. Now there should be laws against using war as a method of arbitrating any quarrel between nations. Soon the American press seized upon the idea and the phrase "Outlawry of War" caught the popular fancy.

Shotwell, besides popularizing the theory, also persuaded French Foreign Minister Aristide Briand that France should get together with the United States and get the ball rolling.

In the United States, public opinion overwhelmingly favored the idea, although hard-headed cynics were inclined to grumble. They sneered and insisted that the pact had no teeth except for the feeble pressure world public opinion might bring about. In fact it was nothing more than a "New Year's Resolution" which would be forgotten before a few months went by. Others suggested that it was nothing more than a "Letter to Santa Claus."

With public opinion, and individuals like Senator William Borah of Idaho (head of the powerful Senate Foreign Relations Committee) behind the idea, it was destined that the thought to "Outlaw War" would be put into the form of a treaty. On August 27th, 1928, with Secretary of State Kellogg signing for the United States, and Foreign Minister Aristide Briand signing for France the peace pact which would come to bear their names was established.

Next the United States and France invited adherence to the Peace Pact by the entire world. At the end run of time sixty nations had signed the Kellogg-Briand Peace Pact and pledged they would "Outlaw War" and not use force against one another.

Although Kellogg was awarded the Nobel Peace Prize for his work, the pact proved to be a gigantic illusion. It was not only deluding but it was dangerous as it lulled the American public into a false sense of security. Instead of outlawing war as it was hoped, the treaty merely outlawed declarations of war. For within little more than a decade almost all of the nations which had signed the pact would be at war fighting each other, thus confirming the doubts of skeptics who had noticed that there were no provisions to enforce the pact if any nation broke its word and went to war. Today the treaty is remembered only as a monument to the naivete of the United States as it became involved in international politics during the 1920s.

Besides this peace pact, 1928 saw the creation of the first colored motion picture. It was exhibited by George Eastman and hailed by almost everyone. Also out of the world of invention came the first successful demonstration of something which was to be called television. The mastermind who discovered how to take an image, break it into light and transport it through the air to a receiver was a man by the name of Vladamir Zworykin. With the new invention going commercial, General Electric built the first television broadcasting station at Schenectady, New York. Its call letters were WGY and on May 11th, 1928, the first programs of scheduled television were broadcast. The first television receivers had an eight inch black and white screen and cost about $3,000.

While these inventive firsts were bringing forth wonderment from the American public, readers were being held captive by the work of Stephen Vincent Benet's novel in verse, *John Brown's Body*, as it became the most widely read poem of the decade. He told the story of the abolitionist hero of the 1850s, evoking fact with myth in his epic poem. Edna St. Vincent Millay also published her collection of poems entitled *Buck in the Snow*, and Eugene O'Neill won a Pulitzer Prize for his drama *Strange Interlude*.

But the person who became a star overnight in the eyes of the American people was the star created by a man by the name of Walt Disney. The star was Mickey Mouse and even though today his creator is dead, Mickey Mouse lives on as a permanent part of American life.

As for the song hits of 1928, most of the country was singing "Makin' Whoopee" and "Button Up Your Overcoat."

As 1929 closed the decade of the twenties, Republican President Herbert Hoover entered the White House. Americans felt comfortable in a pervasive atmosphere of hope for universal peace and prosperity. The country was enjoying boom times, and the unsnarling of the war debts and the reparations tangle seemed to be sparking the flourishing world trade. But all of a sudden people were aghast as they picked up their morning newspapers on February the 15th and looked at a horrifying sight of slain gangsters in a garage in Chicago, a scene that would be labeled the "St. Valentine's Day Massacre."

Ever since the day when prohibition went into effect, the underworld began to grow fat on the sale of illicit liquor. Within months after the passage of the Eighteenth Amendment, a crook by the name of Johnny Torrio, who lived in Chicago, had his boss "Big Jim" Colosimo shot to death. Using his former boss's organization of hoodlums, breweries, and distilleries, Torrio quickly took control of Cook County, Illinois as his feudal domain. But Torrio soon found out that others felt that they had a claim to the same territory, especially one Dion O'Banion, an ex-altar boy. He moved in on the North Side of Chicago, while the Six Genna Brothers (known as the Terrible Gennas) moved in on the West Side. Then "Polack" Joe Saltis and his sawed-off shotgun experts moved in on the South Side. To Torrio things were getting too crowded, so to make sure he would not be muscled out by the others, he imported a young man by the name of Alphonse Capone from New York City to be his enforcer. The job of an enforcer is to wipe out anybody who gets in his boss's way and with no questions asked. Capone had come up the hard way in New York City, participating in street fights, petty thefts, warehouse heists, and two murders.

The fight for control of Chicago started when O'Banion tipped off prohibition agents about a Torrio shipment of beer from a warehouse. Torrio was acquitted of the charge, and then ordered his enforcer to strike back. O'Banion had his headquarters at a flower shop on North State Street. One day three men entered the store. O'Banion recognized them, smiled and went over to shake their hands. As he shook the hand of the first man, the gunsel held on tightly to O'Banion as the other two drew guns and shot O'Banion dead.

O'Banion's successor was Hymie Weiss and he swore vengeance. Within the next few months, Torrio was shot. He recovered from the attack on his life and decided then and there to retire. In 1925 at the age of 45, he sold his interests to his former enforcer Al Capone and moved to Italy.

That did not stop Weiss, for he knew he had to get Capone before Capone got him. On the afternoon of September 20th, 1926, Weiss sent out his gunmen to get Capone. In eight touring cars, the deadly battalion moved in and raked Capone's headquarters at the Hawthorne Hotel with machine guns. With all of this flying lead, it was a wonder that no one was killed. Capone hugged the floor of the hotel restaurant and emerged with nothing more than flecks of dust on his hand-tailored suit.

Capone retaliated. Weiss paid for his attack with his life, and so did Schemer Drucci who succeeded Weiss. All in all, by 1927, 227 mobsters had been slain in gangland wars.

Then because of the heat from federal authorities, Al Capone decided to take a vacation from Chicago and went to his Florida villa, a 25 room bayside palace at Palm Island. While Al was out of Chicago, Buggsie Moran, who took over the old O'Banion interests after the death of Drucci, decided to muscle in on Capone's sacred territory. Then from Florida Capone gave the orders that Moran and what was left of O'Banion's gang be hit and rubbed out.

So Frank Nittie, Capone's enforcer, planned the hit. Members of Detroit's Purple gang were brought in as were men from the Kansas City mob. All were good hit men.

First the gang purchased an automobile that looked like the cars used by the Chicago Police Department. Next, an artist was hired to paint a Chicago Police Department decal on the car doors and then a siren was mounted on the fender so that when the vehicle was finished, one could not tell the difference between the Capone mob's automobile and a legitimate police car.

Then the gang staked out Moran's headquarters, which was a garage where he and his boys met before they went out to pick up the shipments of booze. When all of Moran's men were at the garage the finger men would place a call to the Capone mobsters and then the action would start.

The day the booze shipment arrived was February 14th, 1929, St. Valentine's Day. It was snowing out and this made it difficult for the finger men to make sure all of Moran's men were in the garage. They were able to identify everyone but Moran. Where was he? The fact was that Moran at this time was having a knock-down-drag-out fight with his wife and was late in leaving for the garage at 2122 North Clark Street. While Moran was fighting with his wife, a person who looked like Moran walked down the street and went into the garage. He was about Moran's build and since it was snowing out, a mistake was made by Capone's finger men. They notified the mobsters that everyone was there. Capone's hit-men now went into action. Dressed in the uniforms stolen from the Chicago Police Department, they got into their phony police car and headed towards Moran's place.

They rolled up in front of the garage on North Clark Street at 10:30 A.M. and barged in as if they were making a raid. With guns leveled at Moran's seven men, the order was given to them to face the wall. With their faces to the wall, Moran's men could not see the killers who now came in with machine guns. Momentarily there was a blaze of gunfire and all of the men facing the wall were cut down by the withering cross-fire. Instantly, they were lying on the floor either dead or dying. To make sure no one recovered, the shotgun men next poured a load of O-O (double-O) buckshot into each man on the floor. With their deed done the mobsters left, and Moran's gang was done for. The only man missed was the one Capone most wanted dead . . . Moran. Moran escaped Capone's wrath only because he was arguing with his wife.

Moran left Chicago "for his health," as he put it, and managed to last all through the gangland wars which followed in the next two decades, as the

Victims of the St. Valentine's Day Massacre, on Chicago's North Side.

Syndicate took over the running of crime. He finally died of old age in 1957.

As for Capone, the Internal Revenue Department of the United States Government finally put him away in prison for income tax evasion. He wound up at Alcatraz Federal Prison and in the late 1930s was released; not because he had finished his time, but because he was a dying man. He was dying of the venereal disease, syphilis. By the time he left prison, the disease had lodged in his brain and he came out a vegetable. He died almost unnoticed in 1947 at the age of 48 at his estate in Florida.

As for the St. Valentine's Day Massacre, it too had great significance. The American public became incensed at what a gangland king could do on a whim or impulse. If he could kill these men with impunity, what safety would there be for anyone? These gangsters had to be put away! So now with the public behind them, law enforcement officers really started getting results in their fight against crime, since the men in blue cannot enforce the laws of the land any more effectively than what the citizenry is willing to back and support them.

Al Capone shown on the right, attending the Notre Dame and Northwestern Grid battle, at Chicago. Capone probably was seeking a diversion from his troubles with income tax violation charges. (Former Alderman A.J. Prignano is on the left.)

Besides all of this gangland business, 1929 also saw Sebastian Lando (an inventor) receive a patent for a coin-operated vending machine. Who would have guessed then that those machines would become a way of life for future generations of American people?

Also of interest was the fact that Miss Margaret Sanger was arrested for giving out information on birth control. Yet today, the things for which she preached are common knowledge and everyone seems to know that "The Population Bomb is Everybody's Baby."

Then too, Robert E. Byrd, who flew over the North Pole in 1926, now flew over the South Pole. Thomas Wolfe's masterpiece *Look Homeward Angel* was being widely read, as was Ernest Hemingway's *Farewell to Arms* and William Faulkner's *Sartoris* which was the beginning of his famous saga of Yoknapatawpha County. Indeed, almost all historians and literary critics alike agreed that the 1920s produced a literature that no era since has been able to match.

But the earth-jarring news to come out of 1929 took place in October when the Stock Market crashed and brought an end to the prosperity and good times Americans felt would last forever. Calvin Coolidge must have thanked heaven that he had chosen not to run for President in 1928; and Al Smith, who had been defeated by Herbert Hoover for the Presidency, must have felt like a man who had just missed getting aboard the *Titanic*.

Margaret Sanger shown with other defendants at a hearing on charges of maintaining a birth control clinic in violation of the law.

One could hardly walk a block in the United States without noticing changes after the crash of the Great Bull Market. Women's skirts came down with the stock prices. Dresses for daytime were longer and evening dresses swept the ground as a measure of formality was gradually returning to life. No longer was it the desire or ambition of the American woman to be a red hot baby who by being "Modern" meant that she would be burned out and cynical by the age of 30.

As 1932 approached there was no denying that the old order of the 1920s was giving way to the new era of the 1930s. Soon the mists of time would soften the outlines of the twenties and people like yourselves who look back through history to this era may smile at the memory of those charming, crazy days when radio was a thrilling novelty, and girls wore bobbed hair and knee-length skirts, and a transatlantic flyer became a god overnight, and when common stocks were about to bring us all to a place called Utopia. But when looking back into that era, one should never forget the frustrated hopes, the disillusionments and the scandals when they remember the good old days of THE ROARING TWENTIES.

Chapter 5

THE CRASH OF THE BULL MARKET

The Great War is over and the boys are back home. Wilson and his League of Nations has been scrapped as the United States has just elected Warren G. Harding as President and the country is now returning to what Harding called "Normalcy." Many businessmen and economists predicted that a depression would now take place at the end of the war, as it was felt that Europe would repatriate its gold, war industries would close down, servicemen would be a glut on the labor market and America would return to the recessionary climate of 1913.

It was true that war industries did suffer, but pent-up consumers bought all the products they could lay their hands on and this took up the slack in the market. Europe's needs for American capital goods was as great as its earlier demand for munitions had been. The soldiers who did come home did not find breadlines on their return; instead, they discovered that the economy was suffering from a labor shortage. Furthermore, Germany, which had been crushed by the war, could not be expected to revive for almost another decade. Britain and France, the winners, were economically exhausted. Both had lost many foreign markets during the war, and the United States had captured them. Indeed the United States had profited enormously from the great conflict.

Yes, there was great prosperity throughout the country. American cities were growing rapidly, while at the same time mechanization enabled the farmers to produce more foodstuffs than ever before. The United States had attained the upper hand economically and was now the leading commercial power in the entire world.

Thus, the background to the "Roaring Twenties" had been set in an atmosphere of easy money, permanent prosperity and tremendous growth. This vision of growth and prosperity would become the text of many speeches by businessmen as well as government officials from 1921 to 1929. They could, with reason, observe that this was the greatest growth period in American history, a time of qualitative and quantitative change. Optimism seemed justified, thus the bull market (or buyers market) on Wall Street which began in 1921 did not appear unreasonable to those who participated in it. Flaws were seen by a few but these were minor points when set

106

alongside the great gains of this unusual era.

When asked to list the most important discoveries of the 1920s, business-men mentioned cellophane, celluloid, anti-freeze, oleomargarine, bakelite and rayon. All made their impressions, but none was vital to the economy of the twenties.

On the political scene three Republican administrations worked toward lower tax rates, a budgetary surplus (to help pay off the national debt) and a favorable balance of trade. Presidents Harding and Coolidge were content to allow matters of fiscal policy to be decided by Secretary of the Treasury Andrew Mellon, who was called the greatest Treasury Secretary since Alexander Hamilton. Mellon was one of the most influential members of the government, as it was later said that three Presidents served under him. In private life he was the head of the powerful Mellon clan of Pittsburgh, influential in aluminum, banking, petroleum and other businesses. He was one of the richest men in the world, and could scarcely be expected to do anything that business during the 1920s would oppose. As Secretary of the Treasury, he cut expenditures for almost every department of government, showed a surplus of money each year and paid off a substantial portion of the national debt. He provided an atmosphere of stability which Wall Street greatly appreciated.

Secretary of the Treasury Andrew Mellon, shown at the swearing in of a new Controller of Currency, John W. Pole. To the right is a Chief clerk who administered the oath of office.

Andrew Mellon was also responsible for pushing tax reductions through Congress. Everyone seemed to benefit. As one member of the Senate commented, "Under the terms of Mr. Mellon's tax bill, Mr. Mellon himself gets a large personal reduction of taxes. So large in fact that it totals more than all the taxpayers of the State of Nebraska will get." Yes indeed! Andrew Mellon became the Fairy Godfather of the Bull Market.

By 1925, all the peace treaties were signed and ratified. The Washington Naval Disarmament Conference had resulted in a series of agreements in which most major nations accepted partial disarmament, and the Dawes Plan of 1924 seemed to set Germany's war reparation payments on a realistic basis. Americans loaned Germany sufficient funds to make the first payments, and from that time on, this served as the major financial bulwark for Germany. By 1925, Germany and other European nations signed the Locarno Pacts, which signified the acceptance of the western boundaries drawn after the Great War. Germany also entered the League of Nations, and Russia seemed incapable of exporting her revolution to the rest of Europe. Insofar as the international scene was concerned, the world seemed about ready to enter a new period of history. America felt that she could return to her prewar isolation and concentrate on domestic problems.

On the financial scene, J.P. Morgan and Company was still the bulwark of prestige and power on Wall Street, while Kuhn, Loeb and Company was retaining its perennial second place position.

There was a demand during the 1920s for new securities, so great a demand that stocks were being traded at premium shortly after being offered publicly. The rush was on to get in on the ground floor of any good stock, and any stock was good! There wasn't a bear in sight during most of the twenties. A bear is one who has a pessimistic view of the stock market and the economy, and expects prices to fall. A bull has an optimistic view, and expects prices to rise. To make a profit from the fall of stocks, a bear will usually sell short; borrow shares of stock from a stock owner for a fee. He now sells the stocks he has borrowed, hoping that the market will drop. When the market value of the stock had dropped to what the bear considers a sufficient point, he will buy back the same stock he sold at the lower price and return it to the owner. In the meantime, the bear has made a nice profit!

But now in 1926, even the most dour bear was converted into becoming a bull. The fundamental economic law of supply and demand was most apparent on Wall Street. When the demand for a security exceeds its supply, the price of the security rises. By the midtwenties there was a great demand for securities in America, a demand that far outstripped the supply of stocks. Overnight new companies were formed with little or no backing. The stocks and bonds, regardless of their authenticity or worth, were grabbed up by eager speculators even before they were announced. Most stocks sold at a premium minutes after being subscribed for by those lucky insiders who were able to buy the stocks at the first offering price. It is no wonder then that investment bankers competed with one another for the favors of the businessmen who might want to float a new stock issue or borrow through bond flotations. Money was cheap, stocks and bonds were dear. It was the golden age for those who had the intelligence, imagination and daring to take advantage of the situation and make use of the law of supply and demand.

By 1927, there was a chaotic jumble of companies, flotations, amalgamations, and manipulations and almost all speculators of the twenties used the principal of leverage. To put it simply, leverage involves the ratio of equity that you own in a stock as compared to the debt you owe on the stock. If a person owned a security outright, he was not using leverage. Should he borrow money for the purchase of stock, then he was utilizing leverage. Hence, an individual who resorted to broker's loans or margin money (someone else's money) to purchase stock was using a leverage. Without the ability to borrow and a market in which to sell debt obligations, few corporations could survive in the American environment, since it is a vital aspect of our economy.

As speculation intensified and more and more people purchased stocks on margin so as to gain leverage, the demand for broker's loans rose rapidly. This led to an increase in the interest rate and this in turn attracted money from investment trusts and banks across the nation. The money was loaned to speculators who used it to purchase shares of stocks in the same investment trust that had loaned them the money originally. This created a strange situation. Stock purchases in American companies were made with money loaned by the companies themselves. As the demand increased, the price of the stock went up as did the rate of money. This meant the company could show higher earnings which in turn led to still greater demands for the stock, higher rates and so on. It resembled a dog chasing its own tail. Paper values rose without substance and very few persons thought to question the boom in which all made money. Money was being made with little or no real risk. It seemed as if all you had to do was to go to a broker, buy stock on margin, and in a week sell that stock when the prices went up and you had made a bundle. Although it seemed money could be made with little risk

109

by purchasing on margin, it could also be dangerous. For example, if you purchased $100 worth of stock on 90% margin, you put the stock up for collateral. This means that what you have paid out of your pocket for the stock is $10. The other $90 has been put up by a broker or bank that has loaned you the money. You agree that if the stock which is worth $100 drops below $90, you will make up that margin of difference. Let us assume that the value of the stock now drops to $80. The bank has the option to call on you to come up with the $10 because that is the margin of difference between their $90 loan and the $80 value of your stock. If the bottom fell out of the market and you could not get rid of your stock, you would be obligated to pay the difference of the margin on the stock, even if it meant selling your home. But all that was impossible, as economist Irving Fisher said, "The economy has reached a permanent high plateau."

So the American people had stumbled onto the permanent plateau of prosperity. The bulls were everywhere and they optimistically brought with them a profitable future. This trend seemed to lift the prices to an even higher plateau. This was the year when Henry Ford introduced his Model A, talking motion pictures started with the movie "The Jazz Singer," Babe Ruth hit 60 home runs, and Charles A. Lindbergh flew by himself from New York City to Paris. The market advanced and saw volume expand almost 128 million shares over the 1926 figures.

By 1928, the enormous confidence in the Coolidge prosperity had lifted the price of stock to what many hard-headed financiers considered alarming levels. But if they were alarmed in February, they must have been horrified by March, because the market was still going up. Stories of fortunes made overnight were on everyone's lips. Broker's branch offices were jammed with crowds of men and women watching the shining transparency on which the moving message of the ticker tape was written. It made no difference if you held even a single share of stock, there was a thrill in just seeing the news of that upward trend.

By 1929, it seemed as if the stocks were going out of sight. Time and time again economists and forecasters had cried "wolf, wolf," and the Federal Reserve Board had expressed fear of inflation. Was business in danger? Nonsense, factories were running at full blast and the statistical indexes registered first class industrial health. Well, what about overproduction? Nothing to worry about; business concerns were holding their own and commodities were selling as usual.

Then as always, booms turn to bust. On October 24th, the market which had been having up and down fluctuations, started a downward trend.

110

Mounted police help keep Wall Street crowds moving on October 24, 1929. Many of those in the crowd were wiped out by the severe price decline.

On that momentous Thursday, stocks opened moderately steady in price, but the volume was enormous. Kennecott appeared on the tape in a block of 20,000 shares and General Motors 25,000 shares. The pressure of selling orders was becoming disconcertingly heavy, and as one sells the market looks for buyers. When there are no buyers, the sellers of the stock lower their prices in hopes of finding a buyer. Down, down went the prices. Before the first hour of trading was over the tape was running behind. In brokers' offices all over the country, tape watchers looked at one another in astonishment. Where on earth was the torrent of selling orders coming from?

Fear did not take long in coming. As the price structure crumbled there was a sudden stampede to get out from under. By 11 A.M. traders on the floor of the Stock Exchange were in a wild scramble to sell at market value. Long before the ticker tape could tell what was happening, word had gone out by telephone and telegraph that the bottom was dropping out of things and so the selling orders doubled in volume. Stocks were dropping, not at one point at a time, but at five and ten points at one time. U.S. Steel opened at 205 and before long had crashed to 192. G.E. opened at 315 and had already dropped to 283.

Across the nation, as men and women walked into their broker's office during their lunch hour to see how their stocks were doing, they looked at the big board and the figures took their breath away. Then in an instant, they became aware that the figures they were reading were unreliable. The figures were changing so fast, they saw Westinghouse slide from 189 to 177 in a matter of minutes. They read the figures aloud in a mumbling expressionless monotone voice as their faces grew pale. People now occupied every seat on the floor and stood packed at the rear of the room. A crowd rushed to the visitor's gallery overlooking the Stock Exchange floor. There, the spectators witnessed bedlam. Some onlookers wept, others screamed, while brokers themselves were in tears and hoarse from shouting. The gallery was closed at 11 A.M. to keep the hysterical from starting a riot. By that time over 9 billion dollars in paper values had been wiped out.

In past panics, J.P. Morgan had taken charge, and his reputation and skill had always stilled the fears. But Morgan was dead now and his son who was running the company was in Europe. The manager of the House of Morgan was Thomas Lamont. Lamont and four other leading bankers now met in the Morgan office at 23 Wall Street. These men were Albert Wiggins, in charge of the Chase National Bank, William Porter of the Guarantee Trust, Seward Prosser of the Bankers Trust and George F. Baker of the First National Bank, who together controlled over 6 billion dollars of assets. They met in Morgan's office for the purpose of stopping this market decline, for if they didn't stop the decline, their own institutions might well go under. Each institution put up about 40 million dollars to shore up the market, in order to make such purchases as were necessary to keep trading on an orderly basis. They would try to steady the prices for the leading securities which served as bellwethers for the list as the whole. Bellwether stocks are stocks whose activities are considered especially meaningful to the Wall Street community. It was a dangerous plan for with hysteria spreading, there was no telling what sort of debacle might be impending.

As the bankers separated, Mr. Lamont faced a gathering of reporters in Morgan's office. His face was grave, but his words were soothing. He siad, "There has been a little distress selling on the Stock Exchange and we have held a meeting of the heads of several financial institutions to discuss the situation." Further he assured the reporters that the market was fluctuating because of technical conditions rather than from any fundamental cause.

At about 1:30 P.M. Richard Whitney, vice-president of the New York Stock Exchange, went on to the floor to make a "few" purchases. Everyone knew that he was allied with the House of Morgan, so he was watched

112

by the other floor traders. He went to the post where U.S. Steel was selling and put in a bid for 10,000 shares. His bid price was $205 per share. That was just $2,050,000 he had spent. Next he went to the other bellwether stock areas and purchased 10,000 shares in each of 15 different stocks.

In the space of a few minutes, Mr. Whitney purchased in the neighborhood of $30,000,000 worth of stock. Purchases of this magnitude were not made by just anybody. Who was doing all the buying? It was clear that Whitney was representing some pool, and if the big boys upstairs felt there was nothing to worry about why should the little speculator? All of a sudden everyone was buying again. Cheers rose thunderously from the floor and word quickly spread to the streets. The market was turning around and prices were heading upward. Most of the stocks that had been at a ten point loss at noon were now in the gain column. At 7:08 P.M. (four hours and eight minutes after the exchange had closed), the ticker tapes throughout the country finally stopped. The last transaction had been recorded. Over 12,000,000 shares had changed hands and in 1929, that was a record. The country had tasted bitter panic and "Black Thursday" (October 24, 1929), which was over, didn't appear to be too disastrous. The bankers' pool had prevented for the moment an utter collapse.

Stocks rose on Friday and Saturday morning and the brief panic seemed over. Most people attempted to bury and forget "Black Thursday."

Toward the middle of the day on Monday, October 28, 1929, prices began to slip again and the rout was underway once more. The losses were terrific, U.S. Steel dropped 17 points, while G.E. fell 47 points. It now became obvious that the bankers' pool which had saved the market Thursday was making a retreat. They had saved the market to unload what they didn't want and now that they seemed to be in the clear . . . let the market fall!

By late Monday afternoon, the tape again began to drop behind. Lights in the brokers' offices and banks burned through the night until dawn. Telegraph companies distributed thousands of margin calls and requests for more collateral to back up loans that people had made in purchasing their stocks on margin. But the worst was yet to come. It came the next day, Tuesday, October 29th, 1929. The big gong had scarcely sounded across the great hall of the Exchange at 10 A.M., when storms of selling orders hit the market. There was very little confidence in evidence by anyone. The volume for the first half hour was over 3,000,000 shares. Huge blocks of stock were thrown on the market for whatever they would bring. Sell at any price! The laboring ticker saw a fearful recession of prices take place. People who had counted themselves millionaires a week earlier now watched helplessly as they became beggars and paupers. No one was thinking of buying; the only orders heard were *sell! sell!* The scene of the floor was chaotic. Machinery was behind on orders. Communication systems were jammed. The dumping continued and a complete demoralization fell over the market. Stock brokers and their staffs were physically and mentally exhausted.

It was a critical day for banks too. Many of the corporations which had loaned money to brokers through the banks in order to get high interest rates were now clamoring to have these loans called in. The banks could either assume the loans themselves and run the risk of going under or they could call the money in from the brokers. Many of the bankers assumed the loans and did not add a money panic to the stock panic.

16,410,000 shares were traded in that day which saw the age of the golden glow burn out, a day that saw economic prosperity turn to drought, and saw the little investors (the everyday man on the street) wiped out . . . lock, stock, and barrel.

The Big Bull Market was dead. Billions of dollars worth of profit and paper profits disappeared. The grocer, the window cleaner, the seamstress . . . all had lost their investments. Every town in the country saw families of affluence drop into debt. Investors who had dreamed of retiring to live on their fortunes, now found themselves on poverty road. An era had ended.

Well, what went wrong? Why did the market fall? Everything had been so rosy. Economists who have since analyzed the crash tell us there were many reasons. (1) Overproduction and underconsumption of capital goods. (2) Artificial commodity prices. (3) Inflation. (4) International financial derangement. (5) A European depression. (6) Speculation. And finally number (7) which was perhaps the most important and profound reason of all . . . the psychological reaction called *fear*.

Prosperity was more than an economic condition, it was a state of mind. The Bull Market had been more than the climax of a business cycle. It had been the climax of a cycle of mass thinking and mass emotion for the American people, the idea of get rich quick! Get something for nothing! There was hardly a man or woman in the United States whose attitude toward life was not affected or changed in some way by the sudden and brutal shattering of their hopes and dreams.

With the bull market and prosperity gone, Americans soon found themselves living in an altered world. It was a world which called for new adjustments, new ideas, new habits, new thoughts, and a new order of values. The psychological climate in the United States changed and the evershifting currents of American life turned to new channels to meet the challenge of the Great Depression.

Chapter 6
THE SAGA OF HERBERT HOOVER

This is the story of an individual who was orphaned at the age of eight in 1882 when his mother died of fever, and who despite this fact went on to get an education, amass a personal fortune as a mining engineer, and devote his life to serving others by accepting the responsibilities that a career in government in public life demands. This is the tragic story of a great humanitarian who did much for all peoples of the world, and who dreamed of making it possible for all individuals to have a better way of life. His dream was shattered by a great world depression, a depression which turned his people against him and ended his public career by dashing it to pieces against the rocks of despair. This is the story of Herbert Clark Hoover, the 31st President of the United States, one of the few men who has ever been really qualified for that high office. This is the saga of a man who loved the the country which had given him the opportunity to prosper; of a kind, brilliant, shy, devoted family man who had never failed in any task he had undertaken and who on October 24, 1929, began an agonizing ordeal which would destroy him.

Herbert Hoover was born in 1874, at West Branch, Iowa. By the late 1870s the grassy praires and Indian trails of Iowa were widening into hard earth packed wagon tracks and in some places the railroad was already in operation. At the Hoover household, as in every other Iowa household in those days, the children had chores to do. They hoed the garden, planted corn, milked the cows and sawed wood for the stove. They groomed their horses and made the repairs which were continually needed on any farm. The house the Hoovers lived in was a small white wooden structure about fourteen feet wide and twenty feet long. It was divided into two rooms, a bedroom where the whole family slept in trundle beds, and a combination kitchen-living room. The Hoovers were simple Quakers who feared their God, and on the Sabbath hospitality came only after reverence for the Divine. There were no books in the house except the Holy Bible, an encyclopedia and one or two books which told the tale of how demon rum was to be overcome.

His parents died when he was eight, and Herbert went to live with his uncle Allan Hoover, where he worked in the fields during threshing time.

The small school house which he attended was located about two miles from his uncle's farm. The walk to school was no easy task, for in the fall the prairie winds with the biting cold of the oncoming winter brought a tingle to his face. The brutal snows in the winter and the dragging mud in the spring made schooling a hard thing to come by. His teacher described him as a quiet, serious, and very shy person. By the time he was fifteen, he was interested in becoming a mining engineer. Then in 1891, to gain more knowledge on the subject, he decided to go to college. But colleges were too expensive except for the new college founded by Leland Stanford. Stanford established his University near Palo Alto, California and provided free tuition for students unable to attend state universities because of their high costs.

Hoover did well on the math portion of his entrance examination but poorly on the other subjects. Nevertheless, he was admitted conditionally to Stanford. His grades were nothing to get excited over, and during his four years at Stanford he never once got an "A." Yet, his work in his chosen field was good enough for the head of the geology department to get him a job during summer breaks.

After leaving Stanford University, Hoover, who was twenty-three in 1897, got a job in Australia as a mining engineer at the Coolgardie gold mine which was about 300 miles from the coast of Australia. There, on his advice, Coolgardie-Bewick, Moreing & Company, invested $500,000 worth of their money on men and equipment for the development of a new mine. It paid off. The company made over $55,000,000 on that investment, and from that time on Herbert Hoover's reputation as a mining engineer was made.

The company then sent him to China at a salary of $24,000 per year. Hoover now felt that he could get married so he asked a young lady by the name of Miss Lou Henry of Monterey, California to be his bride. She had been the only girl geology student at Stanford University when Hoover attended there, and he fell in love with her. He cabled her from China to marry him and she said yes. They were married and their traveling began. By 1901, Hoover had become one of the richest engineers of his time. He sought gold, lead, zinc, copper, and tin, and went to India, New Zealand, the Hawaiian Islands, Egypt, Korea, Russia, France, and Burma. Altogether, he crossed the oceans more than thirty-five times. During this period, the Hoovers had two children, Herbert Junior who was born in 1903 and Allan who was born in 1907. Wherever Hoover went, the family went also.

Hoover finally went into business for himself. He became well known for taking over badly run engineering projects and making them pay. He loved making order out of chaos and bringing efficiency to ventures struck

116

by incompetency, or as many companies put it "bad luck."

By 1914, his personal fortune was about $10,000,000 and at the age of forty he began thinking about seeking a job in public service. As Hoover told one of his closest friends, "Any man who has enough money to give his family a comfortable living, has a moral obligation to do something for his generation." Then in the summer of 1914, war came to Europe.

With war came its ravages. The noncombatants behind the lines in Belgium and France grew hungry. Upon hearing this, Hoover used his influence and prestige to gather supplies of food, clothing, and medical necessities to try to save countless men, women, and children from the horrors of the Great War. On October 18, 1914, two and a half months after the war began, Hoover had organized what became known in history as the Belgian Relief. How many people of Europe survived because of his humanitarian work is difficult to determine, but it is estimated that over ten million civilians were recipients of relief shipments to war-ravaged Europe.

In April of 1917, the United States became involved in the Great War and now Herbert Clark Hoover was called on by his own country to organize its food resources. In little or no time at all he became known as the "Food Czar" for he organized the food effort in the United States with such efficiency, that during World War I America produced enough food not only for the United States troops and the American people on the home front, but for most of the people in Europe as well.

With the war over, Hoover went back to Europe. The continent was in shambles and its people were faced with pestilence and famine. Hollow-faced people passed by empty shops and funerals became a familiar sight everywhere. Children did not play in the streets nor did they smile. The fact was that Europe had exhausted itself in the Great War and was almost dead.

At the request of the allied governments of Europe, Hoover took charge of getting food to the war-ravaged countries. He had telegraph lines constructed, railroads put back in running order and had wheat-laden ships emptying their cargoes in harbors which had been smashed by the battles.

For eleven months Hoover did not take a day off and ate on the run. He was driven by the spectre of pale, stunted children stretching out their empty tin canteens and plates for food. As President Wilson put it, "Herbert Hoover's job was second in importance only to the task which faced General Pershing." Herbert Hoover did so much for the people of Europe that in the little country of Finland, the verb "to hoover" meant to be kind and helpful. In Poland, Hoover was honored by a parade of children who carried banners which said, "God Bless Herbert Hoover." And well they should for Herbert

Hoover fed the hungry, clothed the naked, warmed the houses, and gave shelter to all who needed his help. Indeed, he became known throughout the world as "The Great Humanitarian."

Hoover returned to America thinking that the old world of Europe and the new world of America would never understand each other. To explain this, he wrote a book entitled *American Individualism*. The book told how he felt Europe's old hatreds would slow down its progress. Americans on the other hand, Hoover said, had grown away from their European ties for 300 years and had developed their own unique way of life. Two main catch phrases grew from this book. One was "The American Way of Life" and the other was "Rugged Individualism."

But if Hoover thought he could retire from public life, he was wrong. The cry of 15 million starving European children called him back into public service. The American Relief Administration, which was still feeding people all over the world, was running out of money, and Hoover threw himself into collecting money from private sources so that the hungry could be fed. In one night at an affluent dinner in New York City, he collected over $3,000,000. Even Nicolai Lenin, master of the new Communist government in Russia, appealed to Hoover to aid his starving people; because of Hoover's aid over 18 million Russians were saved from death and starvation.

By 1921, Hoover had done all that he could and once again tried to return to private life. In fact he was offered a million dollar a year salary if he would go to work for Daniel Guggenheim and Brothers, which was one of the largest mining firms in the world. But at the same time he was asked by the newly elected President, Warren G. Harding, to join his cabinet as Secretary of Commerce. So once again Herbert Hoover left his home at Stanford University and went to live in a brick house on "S" Street in Washington, D.C.

Hoover took the job and excelled in the position, but was overshadowed in the cabinet by the legendary Secretary of the Treasury, Andrew Mellon. As Hoover went about his work cutting down on government waste, he warned President Harding that many of his friends were using him for their own personal gains and that they were dragging down the President's good name by stealing from the government. At first President Harding just pooh-poohed the stories told him by Hoover, but in June of 1923, Hoover and his wife were asked by Harding to join the President's party which was enroute to Alaska to dedicate McKinley National Park. When the Hoovers joined President Harding at Tacoma, Washington, they found him on the verge of a nervous collapse. At long last the facts that Hoover and others had told the President about his friends were beginning to sink in. The President began to comprehend the gigantic graft and stealing his "friends" were doing. On Hoover's advice, the President decided that the best course of action would be to air the entire scandal publicly when they got back from Alaska.

Once back from Alaska, the President took ill and before he could make public the scandals, he died of a blood clot. It was Hoover's unpleasant task to notify the press that the President was dead, and it was he who telephoned Secretary of State Hughes and told him that the Vice-President must be sworn into office at once. Calvin Coolidge was visiting his father in Vermont when a messenger came chugging up the old dirt road in a car to tell them of the news that the President was dead. Coolidge's father, who was a rural justice of the peace, swore his son into office as the 30th President of the United States in a shadowy house lighted by a kerosene lamp.

Most of Harding's old cronies left the government after his death. Some went to prison but many who had looted the government inexplicably got off. To stabilize the government, Coolidge retained only the most trustworthy men of Harding's cabinet to help him run the country. Naturally Hoover was asked to stay on to help Coolidge get through the scandals of the Harding Administration when they broke loose.

Once the scandals had run their course, Hoover found that he was needed in the government more than ever, as Coolidge hardly did any work at all. Coolidge napped in the mornings before lunch, dozed a bit after eating, then would lay down for a few minutes prior to dinner and never seemed to say anything. In fact, his taciturnity won him the nickname "Silent Cal." In the summers, Coolidge would leave Washington, D.C. and go fishing, yet despite all of this, the Coolidge years from 1923-1929, saw the American economy grow, thanks to the work of others. Almost everyone was getting rich overnight in the magnificent bull market. This was the day when blue-collar workers went to work in a car, Jack Dempsey made $ 5000 a minute for fighting, and radio, the new miracle of the age with its "cat's whiskers" and crystals, brought the remotest parts of the United States together with the flick of a switch. It seemed to foreigners that Americans made millions on the stock market, danced the Charleston and Black Bottom, dodged gangster's bullets in the big cities, wore raccoon coats and carried a hip flask filled with an illegal beverage to drink while "Flapper," "Saxaphone," "Jazz Age," "Bathtub Gin," and "Speakeasy" were the key words of the era.

As 1928 rolled around, the big question was "Would Silent Cal take another whack at the Presidency?" Would he run for another term? Coolidge never really seemed to care about the Presidency. Seemingly, the most important thing in his life was his son Calvin Junior. Calvin Junior was sixteen when he developed a blister on his foot from playing tennis. Blood poisoning developed in the blister and when Calvin Junior died, the man who was the leader of 120,000,000 Americans seemed to withdraw from life. As Coolidge wrote in his diary, "When he died, the power and the glory of the Presidency died with him."

In August of 1928, Coolidge gave the members of the press his answer as to whether or not he would seek another term. He said, "I do not choose to run for President in 1928." No sooner had the twelve word statement been released than a flood of telegrams poured into Hoover's household begging him to announce his candidacy. Hoover did, and at the Republican national convention in Kansas City, he was nominated on the first ballot. On election day he slaughtered Al Smith, the Democratic candidate, with one of the greatest victories yet seen in American political history.

On Inauguration Day, he was mistakenly introduced to the vast radio audience by announcer Harry Von Zell as he said, "Ladies and Gentlemen, the President of the United States, Hoobert Heever." After a snicker went through the crowd, the President began to speak. He stated that he had no fears for the future of the country and that everything was bright with hope. But with the turning of the autumn leaves in the fall of the year 1929, the Great Bull Market crashed and almost every person living in the United States saw his hopes and dreams shattered.

All over the country things suddenly became noticeable; things like the slowing down of new car sales, people planning cruises to the Caribbean or anywhere else cancelling their trips, and down the block "For Rent" and "To Let" signs appeared. By the end of the year, many factories in the country went on halftime, and inevitably the worst possible thing happened . . . bank failures. When some of the leading banks of the country went under because they had speculated in the stock market with their investor's money, the pace of the depression quickened as the economy slid downhill more rapidly. Millions of small people lost their entire life's savings; for when their bank failed, it meant that their savings bank passbooks were worthless.

By the end of 1929, the depression had spread from the east coast to Chicago. There teachers went without pay for months and tax collections had come to a halt. In New York City some of the philosophers of the day looked at the empty skyscrapers, felt that these buildings would stand empty for decades, and that people of the future would compare them to the pyramids of Egypt and structures from Greek and Roman times.

As for President Hoover, he did not lose his nerve when the crash came. The fact of the matter was he had been expecting something like this to happen for a long time. He had warned the Federal Reserve Board as early as 1925, when he was Secretary of Commerce, that it was sheer folly to permit speculators to run wild with purchases of stock on 90% margin, which meant that a person could buy a dollar's worth of stock with a dime.

How bad would this depression be? How long would it last? As far as the Secretary of the Treasury Andrew Mellon was concerned, depressions were part of the system. Why, there had been depressions during the Presidencies of Jefferson, Monroe, Van Buren, Buchanan, Grant, Cleveland, Roosevelt and Wilson. Booms sooner or later turned to busts. It was part of the system and the system should not be tinkered with. For people living during the time, what Andrew Mellon said made good sense. That is the way it had always been. Depressions always came along and purged the rottenness out of the system. High costs and high living would come down and to get out of the depression, people would have to do as they had done in the past, resort to rugged individualism, work harder and live a more moral life.

By the spring of 1930, the nation was still sliding deeper and deeper into depression. Montana ranchers were now killing their herds of cattle because it cost them more to feed the animals and to send them to market than the price they would get. And in the cities when a rare "Men Wanted" sign would appear in front of a factory, police had to be called out to hold back the crowds of jobseekers.

President Hoover did not sit idly by, but on the contrary, he set up what was called the President's Committee for Unemployment Relief. It was made up of thousands of local municipal groups who worked together to see to it that no one in the country went hungry. The committee also called upon the states and counties to take a bigger lead in working out relief programs. The federal government would act as a coordinator but would not take the role of funding local relief programs. President Hoover felt that the federal government should not become involved in local matters. And besides, prosperity was just around the corner anyway.

For a while it looked that way as by early 1931, a year and a half after the crash, industrial production was up, payrolls and stocks were on the rise and unemployment showed signs of decreasing. Could it be that the depression was over? Then, just before prosperity could settle in and take root, an economic hurricane moved in and blew all the best laid plans and dreams away for what seemed an eternity. The economy of Europe began to collapse entirely. As Europe's economy began to sink, it sucked the United States down with it. Ever since World War I, Europe had depended upon American money, American loans, American purchases and the free spending American tourists. After the 1929 crash, all of that faded away and European economies started a downward spiral. Additionally, European countries still had to pay back the United States the huge sums of money which they had borrowed during World War I. Each year European countries who owed the United States money, made a payment and by 1986 . . . yes . . . 1986, their debts and interests would be paid off. It was during this time of economic disaster that the European countries began to refer to the United States as "Uncle Shylock" instead of Uncle Sam.

President Hoover came up with a stunning move which he felt would help the world's economies. He suspended the payment of European war debts for one year. It was called a moratorium. All of a sudden "Uncle Shylock" was hailed as the greatest country on earth by Europeans and Hoover was hailed as a humanitarian with this greatest act of international relations since the Armistice. President Hoover hoped that the moratorium would give the nations who owed us money a chance to recuperate. In fact, it might just well be, that with some of this excess money they had, Europeans might purchase some goods from American industries. But the moratorium accomplished nothing. Foreign buying in America did not take place. The hope that the moratorium would help us as well as the Europeans was now replaced with hopelessness. Moreover, the European nations never bothered to resume payment on their debts after that. Only little Finland ever honored her obligation.

By the summer of 1931, prosperity was not just around the corner anymore. In fact, the worst was yet to come as the country slipped even deeper into the pits of despair and depression. More and more factories were shutting down and more and more people were becoming unemployed, dispossessed, and transitory.

Hoover pleaded with the American people to remember their great heritage, their moral fiber, their self-sufficiency, their pride and self-respect. What they should do was to use their rugged individualism to get themselves out of this depression; the same rugged individualism that drove their forefathers across the plains in covered wagons and forged an empire — the United States.

But Hoover was no Teddy Roosevelt or Woodrow Wilson, and he did not have the eloquence, fire or charisma they possessed to inspire people.

122

The American people were losing their belief not only in their President but in their government as well. To the people, it seemed that Hoover cared more about foreigners than his own countrymen. The crisis was now moving into the realm of the psychological as fear kept spreading.

By now breadlines operated by church groups, hospitals, rescue missions, and the Salvation Army were in every major city. Even gangster Al Capone, to bolster his image, had a soup kitchen open in Chicago. Men stood in lines in all kinds of weather and were grateful to get some beans, stew, bread, and coffee.

Hardly a day went by without at least one family or another being evicted from their home. In the cities, families would sit numbly on a couch on the sidewalk and hope that passers-by would put a nickel or dime in a pot sitting on the family kitchen table.

By the fall of 1931, the President dined alone, in silence and in deep concentration. He was convinced that fear was the villain holding back the country, it was also some of the old outmoded ideas on how to run the economy that needed changing. The government could not sit back as an idle, indifferent spectator while the depression ran its course, it had to do something!

The nation now vented its anger on the Secretary of the Treasury, Andrew Mellon. Mellon had been hailed in the early 1920s as the greatest Treasury Secretary since Alexander Hamilton, and had been called the "Fairy Godfather" of the Bull Market. Everyone in the country felt that as Secretary of the Treasury for Harding and Coolidge he was the man who was behind the nation's great prosperity; and now as Treasury Secretary under Hoover, the people blamed him for the depression.

Mellon was now 76 years old, and best known for the two great principles he had adhered to while he was Secretary of the Treasury; economy in government and tax reductions. His scratch signature "A. W. Mellon" matched his build and personality to a "T." He was always cold, seemingly indifferent and withdrawn. But despite this, during the 1920s, everything about him interested the American public. There was his magnificent art collection, gigantic oil holdings, aluminum monopoly, banks, estates, and his one of a kind all aluminum Pierce Arrow limousine. Now all of a sudden, Mellon seemed to be shorn of his wizardry as on January 6, 1932, Father James Cox of Pittsburgh arrived in Washington, D.C., leading 15,000 people in what he termed a hunger march on the Capitol of the United States. When he arrived, he informed the press that he was the mayor of the shantytowns across the country. He was received on the steps of the Capitol building by Representative Wright Patman of Texas. There Patman suggested that Mellon be impeached for high crimes and malfeasance, while the crowd chanted . . .

"Mellon pulled the whistle
Hoover rang the bell
Wall Street gave the signal
and the country went to hell."

President Hoover realized that confidence was needed in the government, so Andrew Mellon left his shattered office as Treasury Secretary and a new, younger man by the name of Ogden Mills took over. With new blood came new thoughts. Suddenly President Hoover softened from his original stand that it was not the government's business to get involved in the economy; to this end he created measures which he felt would begin to relieve the ailments of the economy. The fact is that Hoover was now actually creating many of the programs for which the New Deal of President Franklin D. Roosevelt would be given credit.

To revive industry, Hoover created the R.F.C., the Reconstruction Finance Corporation. Its purpose was to enable the government to lend big business gigantic sums of money to get it back on its feet. That money would eventually work its way down from the top to the working man of the country.

The idea, however, was immediately criticized by almost everyone. Why lend money to big businesses which were responsible for this depression? The people felt Hoover would do better to give the money to America's poor. But Hoover would not endorse any direct aid project by the federal government for charity or unemployment, as he felt that was the job of the state and local governments, not the federal government. "Well then, tell us," went the argument, "why give money to panhandling millionaires?"

The President fought any idea of direct relief as he felt there should be no federal government dole. He reasoned that it would deaden the will to work, put an end to the drive to succeed and would in the long run kill the nation's ability to come back. Rome died as a result of the dole and it appeared that all of Europe was dying because of it too.

Hoover, nevertheless, fought the depression as best he could at every turn. He pointed out to Secretary of the Treasury Mills that the federal government was spending $2,000,000 per day more than it was taking in. If that continued the United States would go bankrupt; and if bankruptcy came it would bring hideous inflation as in Germany in the early 1920s

124

when wheelbarrows of German marks were needed to purchase a loaf of bread. He really believed that prosperity could not be restored by raids on the public treasury. If anything, the way of life as we knew it under the Constitution, would come to an end. Look what was happening in Germany now! Their government was resorting to Fascism. England and France had gone socialistic, and the Japanese were falling under the rule of the military. Yet, on the outskirts of every town in America stood squalid shacks made of tar paper or cardboard which were referred to as "Hoovervilles."

It seemed by 1932 that the world was coming apart at the seams. When political scientists were asked if anything had ever happened like this before in history, the answer they came up with was — yes, a period of time in history known as the Dark Ages; and it had lasted for 400 years.

As the summer of 1932 got underway, politics was the order of the day. But it was also the time of the Bonus Marchers. These were veterans of the Great War who had been voted by Congress a bonus for the service they had performed during World War I. It was known as the Adjusted Compensation Act of 1924, and the bonus the veterans had coming was to be paid in 1945. At that time Congress would appropriate the money to pay each veteran who had seen combat and who had served his country well.

But the veterans were in need of money now! Why wait until 1945? By that time many would probably be dead and buried. Then too, many economists believed that the best way to beat this depression was to put money into circulation and if that was the case, why not pay the vets their bonus now? So, many veterans marched on Washington, D.C. and camped on every green patch of lawn available in the nation's capital.

The House of Representatives voted to approve the money, but the Senate felt that this march by the veterans was a pressure tactic and voted down the idea of appropriating any money at this time. Most of the veterans left Washington, D.C. and went home but many die-hards decided to stay until the money was appropriated. For two months they stayed, while tempers of both the veterans and the officials of Washington, D.C. became strained. Then an incident happened which caused the President to send troops and disperse the remaining veterans. It was done. The same country these veterans had gone to war for and for which many of their comrades had died, was now using force to drive them out of their nation's capital. How ironic and how bewildering.

The depression, the hopelessness, the hatreds, and the anti-Hoover bitterness finally swept the Democrats under Franklin D. Roosevelt into power in the 1932 Presidential elections. In 1928, Hoover had carried forty states for his victory, but now he was stunned to learn that in 1932 he had carried only six. For Herbert Hoover the job of running the United States was over and a new man would come into power to receive the thanks and blessings of history for leading the people of the United States out of the depression.

Washington, D.C. and the nation forgot Herbert Hoover almost at the moment Franklin D. Roosevelt was sworn into office. The years passed and the New Deal of President Roosevelt plowed its course and then disappeared into history. As time went by and prosperity returned after World War II, books began to appear which were written by men who had worked with President Roosevelt and almost all of them admitted that the best programs of the New Deal were those programs which had been laid out by President Hoover in 1931 and 1932.

A generation of new young Americans would grow up thinking that Herbert Hoover was a failure, only to find out on closer examination that history had dealt with him more cruelly than with any man who had ever served his fellow human beings. Today we know that Herbert Hoover was a noble individual who did as much as he could to aid his fellow man. In 1964 he died at the age of 90. He was buried at West Branch, Iowa where he had grown up and where he had learned that self-sufficiency, pride, and rugged individualism were the driving forces which not only allowed him to achieve his greatness but which would enable every person to achieve whatever their heart's desire was . . . *no matter what.*

Sources I used and which you
might enjoy reading

GENERAL SOURCES

Allen, Frederick Lewis, *Only Yesterday* (1931). Mr. Allen was not a historian but a journalist with *Harper's Magazine* and eventually became editor of that periodical. He was a chronicler of his day and wrote a very entertaining and informative account of the 1920s and the people who influenced that age. He also wrote about the 1930s in a book entitled *Since Yesterday*, and then in the 1950s before his death explained his views of the first half of the twentieth century in a book entitled *Changing Times.*

American Heritage, XVI (August, 1965). This volume was a special issue by *American Heritage* on the 1920s. If you have never looked at or read an *American Heritage* periodical, you have missed some of the best written history ever put down on paper. This *American Heritage* special on the 1920s is one of those delights to just sit back and savor.

Carter, Paul. *The Twenties in America* (1968). An excellent book on the period with Mr. Carter giving his readers a picture of the twenties from the view of a scholar who looks back from his vantage point in time (1968) to question the established concepts that the twenties were not as "Roaring" as others have made them out to be. He believes that it was just another period of time like any other, when people were born, lived and died.

Graff, Henry, ed. *The Life History of the United States* (Vol. 10), (1964). This is part of a *Time-Life* series of the history of the country, and this volume is a thumbnail sketch of events of the period. It is well illustrated.

Hicks, John D. *The Republican Ascendancy*, 1921-1933 (1960). Professor Hicks is a scholar and his book shows it. The book is politically oriented, with the author feeling that the Twenties were a quagmire of amusing events from the time of Woodrow Wilson's days in the White

House until the New Deal of Franklin Roosevelt. He feels that the United States made great progress under President Wilson, but then did not get back on the track until President Roosevelt came into office in 1933.

Leighton, Isabell, ed. *The Aspirin Age* (1949). A delightful book covering incidents from 1919-1941. Ms. Leighton has put together some of the most well-written articles by various individuals, about some aspect of life during the period which had special meaning to them. I have used Ms. Leighton's book in my history classes for many years and during that entire time, I have never heard a student say anything critical about *The Aspirin Age*. It is a *must* book. Why? Just for sheer enjoyment!

Leuchtenburg, William E. *The Perils of Prosperity 1914-1931* (1958). Mr. Leuchtenberg's book is another one of those books which everybody enjoys reading. Besides redating the author's views on the era, the book had little vignettes which practically all teachers, professors, and lecturers have borrowed and used.

McGraw-Hill. *"The Golden Twenties."* This has to be one of the best instructional films made on the twenties. In one hour, McGraw-Hill has brought together a political, social, cultural, and economic sketch of the 1920s. When I was teaching United States History in high school, I did not show movies during classroom time. If a student wanted to see a movie, I told him to watch television or go to the theater on his own time. The students had complained that other teachers showed films during their class time, why couldn't I? I finally relented to prove to them that I was not unreasonable and showed one film during the entire year. This was the one.

Murrow, Edward R. *"I Can Hear It Now"* (1957). Volume III of this audio series deals very nicely with the twenties. From real and reconstructed voices of famous people, Ed Murrow and Fred Friendly give the listener a chance to listen to the sounds of "days gone by." The record does more than that, however. It allows the listener to use his imagination to bring to life in his mind what the authors have created in sound. This is so positive a learning device that I have since created some seventy similar type recordings dealing with history and have entitled them (of all things) *"Excursions in History."* For a list of those Excursions completed (if you are interested) please write to me at P.O. Box No. 781, Los Altos, California — 94022.

Nash, Roderick. *The Nervous Generation 1917-1930* (1970). Many of my students at De Anza College find themselves going to the University of California at Santa Barbara to pursue a degree in history, and here is the man they come back to tell me about. In his book, Professor Nash has put together a superb history on how the twenties got their reputation. He tells who the individuals were who wrote about the time and how their views (as seen then) are not necessarily seen the same way today.

Sann, Paul. *The Lawless Decade*, (1957). Most books (including mine) are full of print and let the reader think up the pictures, but Mr. Sann's book has excellent graphics to go along with the printed word. The twenties are well covered and I would recommend this book to any person dealing with the era, as it covers a lot of small items the reader will enjoy reading and seeing.

Schlesinger, Arthur M. Jr. *The Age of Roosevelt: Crisis of the Old Order (1919-1933)*, (1957). Mr. Schlesinger is a well-known historian who has written several books and was respected enough to be asked by President Kennedy to be kind of a resident historian in the White House during his administration (at last a President who understood the value of history). Every historian has certain favorites in history, and Mr. Schlesinger is no different. He idolized President Roosevent (he grew up during his Presidency — who didn't!) and put together this multivolume work. *Crisis of the Old Order* deals with the twenties and the author shows the reasons why the "Old Order" gave way to the "New Deal." This is a very scholarly work with none of the words left out of direct quotes. These were words which might have been shocking in 1957 when the books were published, but today they are part of the common vernacular.

Sullivan, Mark. *Our Times: The United States, 1900-1925.* (1933-1935). Vols. 5 and 6. Mr. Sullivan's six-volume work would be what we in the history circles would call a "contemporary history," as it was written during and immediately after the 1920s. Next to Frederick Lewis Allen's book *Only Yesterday*, Sullivan's works are probably the most widely read popular account of the twenties. But don't just read volumes five and six, the others will give you a vivid picture of how Americans felt on most subjects, and do much to explain how and why the people of the country reacted in the twenties the way they did.

Time-Life — *The Fabulous Century: Sixty Years of American Life.* Vol. III (1969). This series is a pictorial of life in the United States during the first sixty years of the 1900s with a narrative commentary from page to page. If you like lots of pictures with your history (as I do), then these books will do the trick and whet your appetite to read more on the subjects they cover (which is just about everything).

SOURCES AND READINGS FOR
CHAPTER 1

ON THE EIGHTEENTH AMENDMENT

Coffey, Thomas. *The Long Thirst: Prohibition in America* (1975). An up-to-date account of the "Noble Experiment." There is a good presentation leading up to the culmination of the passage of the Eighteenth Amendment and then some hysterical accounts of the events that took place during the "dry era."

Sinclair, Andres. *Prohibition: The Era of Excess* (1962). A well-written down-to-earth book about the individuals who were behind this amendment and why. But Mr. Sinclair doesn't stop with the passage of the amendment, he goes on to show what happened because people still wanted to drink. Mr. Sinclair not only researched and wrote this excellent account of the era but as a "spin-off" from this book he came up with another book on President Harding (one of the few works which had been printed about Harding to that time).

ON THE NINETEENTH AMENDMENT

Catt, Carrie. *Women Suffrage and Politics: The Inner Story of the Suffrage Movement* (1923). Ms. Catt was involved in the movement, as was her mother, and this is her history of the movement as she saw it. Some interesting comments on her contemporaries makes the book worth reading.

Coolidge, Oliva. *Women's Rights. The Suffrage Movement in America 1848-1920* (1966). Ms. Catt viewed the suffrage movement in 1923 (right after the Nineteenth Amendment was passed), but Ms. Coolidge's book has the benefit of many years of hindsight. In comparing the two books, students will find how history and views of history (interpretations) change over a period of years.

ON THE BLACK SOX SCANDAL

Asinof, Eliot. *Eight Men Out* (1963). One usually finds small articles written in periodicals or newspapers on this scandal that almost wrecked baseball. However, in Mr. Asinof's book, he goes into the background of each player, the events in their lives leading up to the scandal, and what happened to the men involved afterwards.

Smith, Dean. "The Black Sox Scandal" in *American History Illustrated XI* (January, 1977). *American History Illustrated* is a periodical which publishes articles about United States history. Unless you have ever submitted an article to be published in a magazine, don't knock the articles that do appear in them, for the editorial staffs of most magazines are very selective about what they print. *American History Illustrated* is very critical as they even rejected one of my "masterpieces" of history (modesty forbids me from going on). Mr. Smith is Director of Publications at Arizona State University at Tempe. His article is very current, well written and covers the scandal thoroughly. No new knowledge is added but it is always refreshing to read another view on a subject you have covered.

Thompson, Lewis and Charles Boswell. "Say it Ain't So, Joe!" in *American Heritage IX* (August, 1958). Another well-written article about the scandal published by *American Heritage*.

ON AIR TRAVEL

The American Heritage History of Flight (1962). By this time you are probably thinking all I read is the *American Heritage*. Well, it's not! But since the periodical is one of my favorites, it is no wonder that I will always direct anybody who is interested in history to this publication. As the title says, the story of flight is very well outlined.

ON THE RED SCARE OF THE 1920s

Coben, Stanley. *A. Mitchell Palmer* (1963). A well-researched book by Mr. Coben who not only traces the Red Scare of the Twenties, but also gives an in-depth study into the man who helped create the hysteria.

Murray, Robert K. *The Red Scare: A Study of National Hysteria 1919-1920.* (1955). Mr. Murray's treatment of the Red Scare is well handled. It gives one the jitters as the same thing happened during the 1950s with

Senator Joseph McCarthy. The conclusions one draws from Mr. Murray's book is that it could happen again in our own time with little or no trouble at all.

ON PRESIDENT HARDING

Adams, Samuel Hopkins, "The Timely Death of President Harding" in Isabell Leighton, (ed.). *The Aspirin Age* (1949). This is one of those selected articles Ms. Leighton chose for her book. A joy to read.

McCoy, Donald R. "The Election of 1920," in A.M. Schlesinger, Jr. and F.B. Israel, eds. *The History of American Presidential Elections 1789-1968*, Vol. III (1971). For the "smoke-filled room" intrigues, Mr. McCoy explains just how and why Harding got the nomination.

Noggle, Burl, *Teapot Dome: Oil and Politics in the 1920s* (1962). If you are interested in one of the major scandals that broke upon the American public after Harding's death, here it is. Mr. Noggle gives you a look at the individuals who helped destroy President Harding. It is the story of greed, a lust for power, and the corrupt use of money to gain that power.

Russell, Francis. *The Shadow of Blooming Grove: Warren G. Harding in His Time* (1968). Mr. Russell wrote his book with the feeling that not enough had been written on President Harding in a positive light, (he was right) and he did his best to cover all the bases about this little talked-of President. It is a fine book well worth reading.

Russell, Francis. "The Four Mysteries of Warren Harding," in *American Heritage* XIV (April, 1963). I suspect that in the course of putting material together for his book (above) Mr. Russell gave us a preview of some interesting facts about President Harding that were to follow in his book.

Sinclair, Andres. *The Available Man. The Life Behind the Masks of Warren Gamaliel Harding* (1965). While doing research on his book on Prohibition, Mr. Sinclair could not help but be taken by this first President of the twenties. So much had been omitted about Harding's character, that Mr. Sinclair decided he should be given a fair chance in history. His book is a treatment of an individual that could have been you or me. Nothing is cut and dried. A person is the way he is because of his talents, his parents his upbringing, his environment and many other factors. Mr. Sinclair gives you the opportunity to meet President Harding and the people around him who influenced his life. If you would like somebody to write about you, you would want it to be Mr. Sinclair as you can (through his work) actually reach out and shake hands with an individual who got in over his head.

SOURCES AND READINGS FOR
CHAPTER 2

ABOUT THE UNKNOWN SOLDIER

Krythe, Maymie R. *What So Proudly We Hail. All About Our American Flag, Monuments and Symbols* (1968). For little known facts concerning the title, this is the book. It was from here that I got my information about the Unknown Soldier. To really appreciate the things of which I wrote, I recommend that sometime during your life rather than going to Europe or a foreign country, you look around at what your own country has to offer. A vist to the Tomb of the Unknown Soldier will leave you with a feeling that cannot be described by any author.

ABOUT THE WASHINGTON NAVAL DISARMAMENT CONFERENCE

Buckley, Thomas H. *The United States and the Washington Conference 1921-1922* (1970). Mr. Buckley gives us an up-to-date approach to the views of the conference and United States policy during the 1920s. He reflects on what happened then because of policies and strikes a note (makes you think) of the policies we are establishing today with other countries.

Millis, Walter. *American Military Thought* (1966). A writer for the *New York Times* before his death, Mr. Millis was considered to be an expert on most military affairs. In his book he looks back (hindsight) and draws the obvious conclusions that those treaties led the United States down the primrose path to disaster.

Wheeler, Gerald E. *Prelude to Pearl Harbor: The United States Navy and the Far East 1921-1932* (1963). Professor Wheeler has taught more students the values of research than any person I know (I was one of them). As an ex-navy man, Professor Wheeler not only enjoyed being with his students but enjoyed his work and writing about the Far East. His view of the conference and the treaties which followed, point out how little the United States understood the world situation of that day when world leadership was first thrust upon it.

ON COOLIDGE

Abels, Jules. *In the Time of Silent Cal* (1969). This is a recent update of President Coolidge and his times. It is rather scholarly with the author giving us the latest thoughts and interpretations on the Collidge Administration.

Stone, Irving, "Calvin Coolidge: A study in Inertia," in Isabell Leighton, (ed.). *The Aspirin Age*, (1949). Here is another one of those selected articles Ms. Leighton chose for her book. A very humorous view of Coolidge.

White, William Allen. *A Puritan in Babylon. The Story of Calvin Coolidge* (1938). This just has to be one of the best books written on the subject of Calvin Coolidge. White, a journalist, seems to have really captured Coolidge in print. His book is the most quoted and if you want to laugh until tears come to your eyes, this is the book to read. A *must* book for reading.

ON THE KU KLUX KLAN OF THE 1920s

Coughlan, Robert. "Konklave in Kokomo," in Isabell Leighton, (ed.). *The Aspirin Age* (1949). An excellent article which gives you a quick glance at how the Klan grew and then what brought about his demise.

Jackson, Kenneth T. *The Ku Klux Klan in the City 1915-1930* (1967). Mr. Jackson's book discusses the growth of the Twentieth Century Klan and its spread throughout the urban areas of the country. He tells how many times merchants were forced to join the Klan or be boycotted and if they were not eligible to join the Klan how they were literally driven out of the towns and cities in which they lived.

SOURCES AND READINGS FOR
CHAPTER 3

Lindbergh, Charles A. *We* (1927). This book was written by Lindbergh right after his historic flight. As a young school boy during the 1930s, I was thrilled by this book and the adventure of Lindbergh's flight and as a matter of fact, I still am.

Lindbergh, Charles A. *The Spirit of St. Louis* (1953). Now much older and no longer idolized as he was during the twenties, Lindbergh, in a calmer atmosphere, wrote the story of his flight; and how he felt about it then and how he viewed it in 1953. There is quite a contrast in his views as he mellowed with age.

Ross, Walter S. *The Last Hero: Charles A. Lindbergh* (1969). In this biography, how does Ross view Lindbergh? In a kindly light, with some criticism. Someone else's view allows one the opportunity to see facts and events that the participant did not always consider noteworthy.

Ward, John W. "The Meaning of Lindbergh's Flight," in *The American Quarterly* X (1958). Probably no other article has been reprinted as much as Mr. Ward's work. Almost every instructor of history has made this required reading for his students and when you read it, you will understand why Charles Augustus Lindbergh was such a national hero.

SOURCES AND READINGS FOR
CHAPTER 4

ON PROHIBITION

Asbury, Herbert. "The Noble Experiment of Izzie and Moe," in Isabell Leighton, ed. *The Aspirin Age* (1949). If you ever wondered what gave color and flair to the twenties, Mr. Asbury's hilarious well-written article is one answer. Hollywood and television would do well to look into the capers of these two prohibition agents for an Emmy-winning series in comedy.

Harrity, Richard. "America on the Rocks; The Wild Story of Prohibition," in *Look*, 33 (January 21, 1969). This article by Richard Harrity is an example of how *Look* magazine enlightened many people about the crazy happenings of the twenties.

ON THE SCOPES TRIAL

Levine, Lawrence W. *Defender of the Faith. William Jennings Bryan: The Last Decade, 1915-1925* (1965). Mr. Levine's excellent work examines Bryan and tells why he was hailed as such a champion of the people during his time. It isn't very often a political party will nominate a person three times as their Presidential candidate, especially if he has lost two times before, but Bryan was a man who received that honor from the Democratic Party. Today most people look back to the "Monkey Trial," shake their heads at the Fundamentalist belief as embodied by Bryan, and ask "How could he be so backwards?" Mr. Levine shows that he was not backward and that even after the trial and before his death (one week after the trial), letters pouring in to Mr. Bryan were all congratulatory, praising him for his stand.

Scopes, John Thomas. *Center of the Storm* (1967). After Scopes left his teaching position at Dayton, Tennessee, he went to work for an oil company from which he retired in 1967. He then wrote his reminiscences of the trial; how he saw things then and how he viewed things in 1967. An interesting book.

Shaw, Bynum, "Scopes Reviews the Monkey Trial," in *Esquire*, LXXIV (November, 1970). Just before his death in 1970, Scopes was interviewed by *Esquire* magazine. The occasion for the interview was the fact that the State of Tennessee finally repealed the law which found Scopes guilty.

ON THE TRIAL OF BILLY MITCHELL

Davis, Burke. *The Billy Mitchell Affair* (1967). In this book on Mitchell the author gives his feelings on Mitchell's crusade for his beliefs. Although the book is well done, I felt the author could have emphasized (in view of the past) what things today we might be aware of in our own generation.

Hurley, Alfred F. *Billy Mitchell: Crusader for Air Power* (1964). Hindsight is one of the greatest things going for any historian. Mr. Hurley writes his book on this view with an excellent background on the events leading up to the court martial, and the trial itself. He then follows out the rest of the life of the man who after having brought disrepute to himself, went on to fight for his beliefs. Good book.

ON AIMEE SEMPLE MCPHERSON

McWilliams, Carey. "Sunlight in My Soul," in Isabell Leighton, ed. *The Aspirin Age* (1949). Mr. McWilliams article on Aimee has some real understanding of this complex person. Rather than condemn her as a charlatan like so many have done, Mr. McWilliams is more gentle in his approach to the interpretation of the historical facts about this wonderful individual. As a matter of fact, so am I.

ON HENRY FORD

Nevins, Allen. *Ford: The Times, The Man, The Company* (1954). Mr. Nevins is a well-established historian and his works are always of the highest caliber. In this book on Henry Ford, he immerses his reader in the times that made the man and his company. Excellent book.

Rae, John B. *Henry Ford* (1969). Mr. Rae was a person who grew up idolizing the Ford "Horatio Alger" story and so his book will reflect just that. Yet, Mr. Rae is also a critical enough author that he is willing to give good criticism of some of Ford's more outspoken stands on issues.

ON SACCO AND VANZETTI

Ehrmann, Herbert B. *The Case That Will Not Die: The Commonwealth vs. Sacco and Vanzetti* (1969). Probably more has been written on the Sacco and Vanzetti case of the 1920s than any other subject of that era. Mr. Ehrmann shows the feelings of the times which convicted the two men, and then how those times and circumstances denied Sacco and Vanzetti the civil liberties that we all take for granted.

ON THE KELLOGG-BRIAND PEACE PACT

Shotwell, James T. *War as an Instrument of Policy* (1929). Since Professor Shotwell was one of the main promoters behind the idea to "Outlaw War," his book makes interesting reading and one only wishes the things for which he fought had come true.

Stone, J.E. *S.O. Levinson and the Pact of Paris* (1943). It was this Chicago man who has been given the credit for the original idea to "Outlaw War." Mr. Stone wrote his book during World War II and his views and criticism of the Kellogg-Briand Peace Pact are not too favorable. It makes interesting reading from today's standpoint since much could be learned from these events in relationship to our negotiations today (i.e. the Salt talks).

SOURCES AND READINGS FOR
CHAPTER 5

Galbraith, John K. *The Great Crash, 1929* (1965). Any time you are in the field of economics, you always consult the works of Mr. Galbraith. As

137

one of the world's foremost economists, Mr. Galbraith's views of what took place when he was a young man are informative. Besides using the tools of his trade to explain the crash, Mr. Galbraith also puts in some of his own recollections.

Sobel, Robert. *The Great Bull Market: Wall Street in the 1920s* (1968). Mr. Sobel's book is one which you can read with no difficulty. He explains every term and the reader can understand even the most complex workings of Wall Street. His coverage of the events leading to the crash and its aftermath is excellent. Recommended reading.

SOURCES AND READINGS FOR
CHAPTER 6

Robinson, Edgar and Vaughn D. Bornet, *Herbert Hoover: President of the United States* (1975). Professor Robinson (now emeritus) has done one of the most scholarly works to this date on one of our most musunderstood and abused Presidents. Since Professor Robinson taught at Stanford University, he had complete access to President Hoover's papers which are located there. A well-written book and excellent reading.

Romasco, Albert U. *The Poverty of Abundance, Hoover, the Nation, the Depression* (1965). Mr. Romasco's treatment of Hoover is not as gentle as others. He feels that regardless of Hoover's background, he should have been able to do more to get the country out of the pits of depression. Good book with a harsh view.

Smith, Gene. *The Shattered Dream* (1970). You'll like this book from the very beginning. Mr. Smith is not a historian, but a free-lance writer and there is a real feeling to his work. The reader finds himself being President Hoover, and from that point, the book is a real eye-opener. Excellent book.

INDEX